GAME OF MY LIFE

SAN FRANCISCO

GIANTS

GAME OF MY LIFE

SAN FRANCISCO

GIANTS

MEMORABLE STORIES OF GIANTS BASEBALL

MATT JOHANSON

FOREWORD BY BRUCE MACGOWAN

SPORTS PUBLISHING

www.skyhorsepublishing.com

10 9 8 7 6 5 4 3 2 1

Library of Congress Cataloging-in-Publication Data
Johanson, Matt, 1970–
    Game of my life. San Francisco Giants : memorable stories of Giants baseball /
Matt Johanson.
        p. cm.
    Includes bibliographical references.
    ISBN 978-1-61321-040-6 (alk. paper)
    1. San Francisco Giants (Baseball team)—History.   I. Title.
GV875.S34J63 2011
796.357'640979461—dc23
                        2011018649

Printed in the United States of America

To all the friendly faces, both in and out of uniform,
who helped along the way.

CONTENTS

FOREWORD

BY BRUCE MACGOWAN

ASK ANYONE WHO IS a baseball fan about a favorite memory of a game, and you're going to get some distinctive and varying responses. My father told me how he went to his first game with his dad in 1927 and saw Babe Ruth, Lou Gehrig, and the New York Yankees at Yankee Stadium. The thing he remembers most about that game was that he caught a foul ball off the bat of a back-up player named Cedric Durst. What a memory for a seven-year-old!

My own personal favorite concerns a Giants game I went to with my mom, dad, and brother at old Seals Stadium back in 1959. By the time kids are six or seven, they usually start paying a little closer attention to what's going on during the games, and so it was with me as I have little recollection of minor-league Seals games I attended with my dad in earlier years. But I remember this particular game: my dad took us out of school on that cool, overcast September afternoon to see the Cubs and Giants play in a key game that had pennant implications. Fighting for their first National League championship in San Francisco, the Giants were racing the rival Dodgers and needed every win they could get. The game I attended with my family that day turned out to be a glorious one for Giants fans. Playing for Chicago, Bobby Thomson (yes, *the* Bobby Thomson) hit the first major league home run I ever saw in person. But the Giants' young southpaw Mike McCormick limited the damage from that point on, going eight and a third strong innings before turning it over to the bullpen. Then San Francisco's "Sad" Sam Jones gave up a pair of RBI singles, and the game went into the bottom of the ninth tied at 3-3.

Batting with one out was Jackie Brandt, an unremarkable player who briefly patrolled right field for the Giants. The soft-spoken Nebraskan, however, would enjoy his moment in the sun on this memorable afternoon. Brandt broke up the contest and sent everyone home happy by belting a low line drive over the right center-field wall. The home run capped an exciting 4-3 win for San Francisco.

Brandt was later traded to the Baltimore Orioles in a deal that brought San Francisco two pitchers, and he finished off his career in 1967 as a back-up outfielder on a bad Houston Astros team. But on that day, Jackie Brandt was the hero of at least one little seven-year-old baseball fan. Out of thousands of games I've seen as a fan and broadcaster, this favorite memory still stands out sharply to me.

Readers will enjoy the many great baseball tales told in this fine book by Matt Johanson, focusing on the special memories of Giants players. Together the games and stories of the players who starred in them comprise an enjoyable history of the team, from an author who, like myself, knows how enjoyable baseball history is.

Bruce Macgowan is a longtime Bay Area broadcaster and sports historian.

1
ORLANDO CEPEDA

"A DREAM COME TRUE"

POSITION: first base, left field

SEASONS WITH GIANTS: 1958–1966

ACCOMPLISHMENTS: seven-time All-Star; won National League Rookie of the Year award in 1958; led National League in doubles (38) in 1958; led National League in RBIs (142) in 1961; inducted into the Hall of Fame in 1999

GAME OF HIS LIFE: April 15, 1958, versus Los Angeles Dodgers

SHORTLY BEFORE THE HISTORIC game started, two of the men who made it possible treated the crowd to a bonus contest. San Francisco's mayor, George Christopher, took the mound to pitch to his counterpart, mayor Norris Poulson of Los Angeles, and the leaders quickly showed amused spectators why they entered politics instead of sports.

Christopher's first throw—it was not a pitch—nearly hit Poulson in the head. The "wild in the wing" mayor then heaved a ball behind his opposite number, and bounced the next one over the plate. When Poulson finally connected, he rolled a dribbler across the infield and tore out of the batter's box at full speed. But instead of running to first base, he gleefully sprinted straight to third.

Roaring in laughter were 23,448 delighted spectators, enough to fill every seat and standing space in Seals Stadium.

Baseball was hardly new to the "city that knows how." Such immortals as Lefty O'Doul and Joe DiMaggio called San Francisco home. The Seals, winner of fourteen Pacific Coast League pennants, had played there since before the great earthquake of 1906. For a time, the city also hosted the San Francisco Sea Lions, a Negro League team.

But San Francisco and the entire west coast had waited decades for big league baseball to follow in the Lewis and Clark expedition's 154-year-old footsteps. When it finally arrived on April 15, 1958, fans in and out of the park were determined to enjoy every minute of it.

"We are going to miss the Seals," Christopher said. "They gave us some great ball clubs, teams that would have held their own in either of the big leagues. But the Seals are gone now, leaving behind a tradition of hustle and fight matched by that of the Giants."

The arrival of the Giants put the city in a frenzy. To welcome their new team, more than 100,000 people attended a downtown ticker-tape parade, wildly cheering the players who drove down Montgomery Street in open convertibles. "Welcome SF Giants. Swat Them Bums," read billboards that sprang up around the city. A downtown clothing store gave women booklets explaining baseball rules and advising them about appropriate ballpark attire. Giants uniforms graced the mannequins of Macy's store windows.

San Francisco raced to adopt a plan to build the team a stadium at Candlestick Point by the 1960 season. In the meantime, Seals Stadium at 16th and Bryant streets underwent a $75,000 upgrade and added 2,600 seats in left field. The flags of the eight National League teams were raised. Tickets sold briskly, starting at 90 cents for the bleachers and reaching $3.50 for box seats. For Opening Day against the equally new Los Angeles Dodgers—the first-ever major league game east of Kansas City—scalpers marked them up to a scandalous $15.

As the mayors performed their comic act and dignitaries shook hands on the diamond, fans in the packed house feasted on concessions. Peanuts, soft drinks and coffee sold for 15 cents. Hot dogs went for a quarter, beer for 35

Orlando Cepeda signed his contract just minutes before the Giants' debut game in San Francisco. *Photo file/MLB Photos via Getty Images*

cents. Thousands of spectators skipped work or school to attend that Tuesday afternoon. In fact, the state Legislature in Sacramento failed to pass its budget that day by one vote because a member of the Assembly was at the game.

The first pitch was just minutes away. But in the home clubhouse, the new Giants first baseman realized that the team had overlooked a fairly important detail.

"I had made the team, but I had yet to sign a contract," recalled Orlando Cepeda, then a 20-year-old rookie learning English. "Believe it or not, in all the hoopla they had forgotten about me." Cepeda told a teammate who called Chub Feeney in the front office. The general manager raced down with the standard papers and $7,000 written in as the salary.

Cepeda grew up in the ghettos and slums of Puerto Rico as the son of baseball star Perucho Cepeda. Known to his fans as "The Bull," Perucho was a slugging shortstop called by some the Babe Ruth of Latin America. But despite his talent, the family lived in poverty.

Orlando became a ballplayer, too, and at age 17, he jumped at the chance to sign a minor league contract with the New York Giants for $500. The Bull never wanted to grapple with racism in the United States, but his son, the "Baby Bull," went to America in 1955. Three years of minor league ball took Cepeda through the segregated South where he and other black players were barred from hotels and restaurants their teammates frequented.

After making the big club, Cepeda had looked forward to playing in New York, where his sister and other relatives lived. He admits that owner Horace Stoneham's decision to move the team to California initially disappointed him. But it didn't take long for Cepeda to change his mind thanks to the reception the club received. It started as soon as the Giants arrived for the first time at San Francisco Airport.

"When I got off the plane some Puerto Rican people were waiting for me," Cepeda remembered. "Some were waving Puerto Rican flags. About 400 fans were awaiting the team at the airport. I was so touched. It was something I had never expected."

Late one night around this time, half-asleep, Cepeda believes he saw his father, who put his arms around him and smiled. The vision comforted the young man far from home and cemented his confidence. "I knew then that things would be just fine," he said. "I was a major league baseball player."

When Cepeda signed his last-minute contract, he began what became a 17-year big league career. The Giants started him along with fellow rookies Jim Davenport and Willie Kirkland in the opener against the Dodgers. Taking the mound for the Giants was Ruben Gomez, also Puerto Rican. Though Los Angeles threatened with two hits and three walks in the early innings, the pitcher baffled the Dodgers with his screwball in the clutch. Thanks to timely strikeouts and ground balls, he escaped without damage.

Los Angeles started ace Don Drysdale, the side-armed sinkerball pitcher who won 17 games in 1957. He quickly dispatched the first six Giants batters, though Cepeda nearly collected the first San Francisco Giants hit in the second inning.

Drysdale started the nervous rookie with an inside fastball. "Drysdale wouldn't give you an inch," Cepeda said. "On more than one occasion, he had me hitting the dirt." This time, the Giant scorched a ground ball to Dodgers third baseman Dick Gray, who robbed him with a clean pick and a rifle shot to first.

In the third, San Francisco loaded the bases on two walks and a single. Ironically, it was Gomez, that day's starting pitcher, who cracked the home team's first hit at Seals, an infield single to third. That brought up the club's new third baseman, Davenport, who would spend a lifetime with the Giants as a player, coach, scout, and manager. On this day, he knocked in the team's first run in its new home with a sacrifice fly to right. Then left fielder Jim King delivered an RBI single.

The Giants might have scored many more in the third but for an amazing play by a San Francisco-born Dodger. Kirkland hit a fly ball high and deep to center. Racing under it was Gino Cimoli, once a star at the city's Galileo

High School. The center fielder stumbled but, on one knee, reached out and caught the ball, and San Francisco settled for a 2-0 advantage.

Giants shortstop Daryl Spencer hit San Francisco's first homer in the fourth, and Willie Mays later hit a two-run single in the rally. Mays lost his cap chasing down a fly ball in the fifth, thrilling the spectators who before then had only read about his prowess. Only years later would the center fielder admit that he purposely wore caps a little too small to produce the flying-cap effect.

By the time Cepeda batted in the fifth, the Dodgers had sent Drysdale to the showers and brought in Don "The Weasel" Bessent from the bullpen. Cepeda worked the count to 3-1, and then attacked the pitch he wanted. The ball flew high over the right-field wall. The crowd cheered madly as Cepeda trotted the bases. "The home run did it for me. It established a love affair with the city of San Francisco," he said. "I had not known anything like this before."

After hitting loud outs all day, Kirkland finally got his due in the eighth with a run-scoring single. Leading in the ninth, 8-0, the Giants' only remaining suspense was whether Gomez could complete the shutout.

After two outs, Los Angeles put two men on base with a walk and a single, bringing up future Hall of Fame shortstop Pee Wee Reese. But Gomez caught him looking at a called third strike. The Giants had started their San Francisco history with a lopsided win over their greatest rivals, to the elation and long-lasting pride of their new hometown fans.

The Game of My Life
By Orlando Cepeda

My first major league game was a dream come true. As a kid, I dreamed that someday I would be a big league ballplayer. To find myself on the field with so many great players, that's a day I will never forget. I was a little nervous, pinching myself, thinking to myself, "Is this for real?"

This used to be a minor league town, and here we are playing the Dodgers in the very first game on the west coast. The people were going crazy, in the city, in Oakland, San Jose, all over the Bay Area. If we had 60,000 seats in the ballpark that year, we could have filled the park every single day.

Drysdale's [first pitch to me] wasn't too nice. It was a mean first pitch. He didn't mess around, and he let me know, "Welcome to the bigs." Bessent fed me a change-up, and I was ready. I got good wood, and the ball sailed 390 feet over the right-field fence. When I hit the home run, I was so happy inside that I didn't hear the fans or anything. I ran the bases like I was rolling. It was incredible.

At that moment, I didn't know the meaning of it, to come here and play ball in '58. But now looking back, that was very nice to participate in the first game on the west coast. I love San Francisco, the Bay Area and the organization. Everyone here has been great to me.

	1	2	3	4	5	6	7	8	9	R	H	E
Dodgers	0	0	0	0	0	0	0	0	0	0	6	1
Giants	0	0	2	4	1	0	0	1	x	8	11	0

Cepeda: 5 at-bats, 1 run, 1 hit, 1HR, 1 RBI

More than 100 sportswriters covered the opener, the most ever for any Giants ballgame besides World Series or All-Star games.

"WE MURDER THE BUMS," screamed the *San Francisco Chronicle* the next morning. The papers documented every conceivable aspect of the contest, from the celebrity attendees' fashion choices to the quality of the hot dogs: "large and tender," wrote Prescott Sullivan, with "mustard a notch above Pacific Coast League standards." Reporting for the *Examiner*, Sullivan also complimented the fans for their "thorough understanding of baseball and with it the good judgment to reserve their excitement for the exciting plays." One writer praised Cepeda for guarding first base "like a tough marine."

Giants manager Bill Rigney commended Cepeda and fellow rookies Davenport and Kirkland for delivering in their debut. "How about those three!" he exclaimed. "Playing like that in their first big league game, it was just tremendous." Together the young trio combined for four hits and three RBIs.

"It was a remarkable opener," recalled Lon Simmons, who debuted himself that day as a big league broadcaster. "It couldn't have been any better than beating the Dodgers and shutting them out and putting on a big show."

Among the only complaints was a scarcity of beer vendors in the upper deck. Also, a two-by-four fell from the roof of the just-remodeled press box, hitting the head of a sportswriter from Eugene, Oregon. But he wasn't badly hurt, and stayed for the game.

As memorable as the game was to the Giants and their new hometown fans, it was equally forgettable for the new Los Angeles Dodgers.

"Outside of getting beat, 8-0, I don't remember very much about that first game," Drysdale later said. "I couldn't worry about the pageantry. I had to pitch."

"Oh, I do remember looking up at the big Hamm's beer glass on the brewery next to Seals Stadium and watching it filling up again and again," the Dodger said. "I was kind of intrigued by it. After the game I had, I could really have used a beer."

Perhaps even more disconsolate were the deserted fans both clubs left behind in New York. A city that used to enjoy three teams was left with only one. Like countless others, television personality Happy Felton was anything but overjoyed.

"I'm heartbroken. I'm sick," he said. "Do you realize that on July 4, with the Yankees out of town, there won't be a major league ballgame in New York?"

The Polo Grounds, the Giants' former home, housed the New York Mets in future years. Ebbets Field, the Dodgers' old park in Brooklyn, hosted college ball, circuses, rodeos, and boxing. Within seven years, both stadiums were demolished.

But in San Francisco, the Giants finished third in the league in 1958 with a record of 80-74, a healthy improvement from 1957. Cepeda played strikingly well, batting .312, clubbing 25 homers, and driving in 96 runs on his way to Rookie of the Year honors. Yet, his eight years with the team weren't always so pleasant.

After the arrival of Willie McCovey in 1959, the two were forced to share time at first base. Cepeda also sparred at times with manager Alvin Dark, who led the club to the 1962 World Series, but also angered players with comments perceived as racist and by trying to ban the team's Latinos from speaking Spanish to each other.

Cepeda and his old skipper have long since reconciled, he said. "Playing with Dark was kind of hard," Cepeda said, "but he told me a couple of years ago that he was sorry for the way he treated black players."

In fact, Baby Bull has come to look differently on many events in his life that were extremely difficult to deal with at the time. After his retirement in 1974, Cepeda spent 10 months at a federal prison in Ft. Walton, Florida for marijuana smuggling. Two marriages failed, he lost his wealth, and struggled with depression. But these painful hardships led him to explore Buddhism, a decision that changed his life and which he now calls "the best thing that ever happened to me."

Cepeda settled in Fairfield, California, with his wife, Mirian. He's worked as a Giants community representative since 1990, visiting Bay Area schools to warn "at-risk" kids about the dangers of drugs and alcohol. Cooperstown summoned him in 1999, and like his fellow Hall of Famers Mays and McCovey, Cepeda enjoys visiting the Giants clubhouse, meeting the new players, and talking about the old days.

"My first game means a lot to me," he said. "When you play ball, you take things for granted. Sometimes we complain, there's too much work, there's too much travel. Now that I'm retired, I know I was very blessed to be born with the skill to play baseball. Every day is a better day."

2

WILLIE MAYS

"DON'T ASK ME HOW I DID IT"

POSITION: center field

SEASONS WITH GIANTS: 1951–1952; 1954–1972

ACCOMPLISHMENTS: 20-time All-Star; won National League Rookie of the Year award in 1951; won National League Most Valuable Player award in 1954 and 1965; led National League in batting average (.345) in 1954; led National League in home runs in 1955 (51), 1962 (49), 1964 (47) and 1965 (52); led National League in stolen bases in 1956 (40), 1957 (38), 1958 (31) and 1959 (27); won 12 consecutive Gold Gloves from 1957-1968; inducted into the Hall of Fame in 1979

GAME OF HIS LIFE: April 30, 1961 versus Milwaukee Braves

EVEN WILLIE MAYS HAD his tough days on the job, like the early hours of April 30, 1961. However, the way the slumping Giant turned a sick day into a career highlight was the kind of feat that made him Willie Mays.

"Everything I hit was going out of the ballpark," Mays said. "What a day. I couldn't believe it."

The Giants arrived in Milwaukee for a three-game series that spring, though Mays didn't look much like himself in the first two contests. Braves ace Warren Spahn, ageless and still fearsome at 40 years old, no-hit San Francisco in the first game. The Giants erupted for 15 hits in the rematch, but Mays was the only starter who didn't get one.

Mays' average dropped to .291, a very respectable mark for most players though well below the standards of the "Say Hey Kid."

"I know they say I'm slumping," said Mays, then a week shy of his 30th birthday. "I'll snap out of it. I'll get me four hits one of these days."

April 30 didn't look like his day to even get four at-bats. During a postgame stroll the night before, Mays and his roommate Willie McCovey passed by a take-out joint and picked up some ribs to take back to their hotel. The two devoured the ribs in their room while watching television, turned out the lights, and went to sleep.

Around 3 a.m., a most unhappy Mays awoke with his stomach turning. He threw up, prompting McCovey to call team trainer Frank Bowman, who gave him a sleeping pill. Five hours later, Mays forced himself out of bed.

"When I got to the park, I felt dead," he recalled. "I certainly didn't feel like playing, but I still got dressed."

Mays figured he needed the day off, though he took some batting practice anyway. To his surprise, the ball jumped off his bat. Out of 15 practice swings, a dozen balls cleared the fence of Milwaukee's old County Stadium.

"After that," he remembered, "there was no way I was going to sit on the bench." Manager Alvin Dark approved Mays' last-minute addition into the lineup.

Braves starting pitcher Lew Burdette threw a good fastball, curve, slider, and sinker. His opponents frequently accused him of throwing a spitter, too. "Burdette always pitched me tough," Mays said. "I never hit him too hard." But when the right-hander threw Mays a slider in the first inning, the Giant mashed the ball more than 420 feet over the left field wall.

Milwaukee wrested the lead back in the home half with a rally against San Francisco's starter "Bugsie" Billy Loes. Two Braves singled ahead of the great Hank Aaron, who socked a three-run homer. Milwaukee took a 3-1 lead, and a long-ball showdown of future Hall of Famers began.

Giants shortstop Jose Pagan, no power hitter, connected against Burdette in the third for his first home run of the year. At that time in baseball history,

Willie Mays tied a major-league record with four home runs in a game on April 30, 1961. *AP Images*

frustrated pitchers were allowed and perfectly willing to retaliate for such indignities, and sure enough, Burdette nailed third baseman Jim Davenport three batters later.

That proved to be a mistake, because it brought up Mays with a runner on base. In the rematch, Burdette threw a sinker and Say Hey abused him again, knocking a two-run shot 400 feet to center. San Francisco swung ahead, 4-3, and Mays marveled that he was hitting the All-Star's breaking stuff as easily as batting practice fastballs.

Loes recovered from a shaky first to retire 14 straight Braves in the middle innings. Meanwhile, even the Giants not named Willie Mays joined in the wild power exhibition. Orlando Cepeda homered in the fourth to knock Burdette out of the game. Milwaukee's Carl Willey came in to replace him, but the onslaught continued, as Felipe Alou knocked one out and Pagan hit another, all in the same inning.

When Mays led off the fifth, the Giants led by 7-3 and the Braves went to the bullpen again, summoning Moe Drabowsky. Mays drilled a screaming liner deep to center. On Mays' first two bombs, Aaron didn't even move as he watched the balls fly over the fence. This time, Aaron played all the way back at the center field wall, jumped, and snared it over the fence, robbing Mays of a third homer. His play wouldn't save the day for the Braves, but by the time the game was over, it cost his rival a major league record.

"I tell Hank all the time, 'If you let it go, I would have got five home runs,'" Mays said. "It was the same thing I would do to him if I got a chance, except that I never did because he always hit them so far."

Another Giants rally in the sixth brought Mays to bat with two aboard. His adversary this time was Milwaukee southpaw Seth Morehead. If pitchers of the era were inclined to bean batters following home runs, they were equally motivated to pitch to the sluggers who hit them. To their credit, Moreland and his fellow hurlers went right after Mays all day.

"They wanted to prove they could get Mays out," said Giants pitcher Bobby Bolin. "They'd rather try to get him out and give up a home run than just walk him intentionally. That ain't much to brag about."

Morehead fared no better than his teammates, but at least he didn't give up a cheapie. He threw a sinker which Mays ripped 470 feet into the picnic area outside the stadium, one of the longest homers of his career. The three-run shot put San Francisco ahead, 11-3.

Aaron answered back in the Braves' sixth with another homer of his own, though "The Hammer" was not destined to win this power-hitting contest. The game out of reach, even Milwaukee fans got behind Mays when he hit again in the eighth.

In the process of using his entire bullpen, Braves manager Chuck Dressen brought in pitcher Don McMahon. The one-time All-Star reliever threw a slider, and Mays smashed the pitch 400 feet over the center-field wall. The crowd of 13,114 shouted enthusiastic approval for the visiting star who tied a major league record with his fourth homer in the game.

Perhaps the only Giant who didn't enjoy the achievement was McCovey, who came behind Mays in the batting order. "I was scared," McCovey admitted. "I was expecting to get knocked down after each of Willie's home runs."

Pitching the ninth, Milwaukee's George Brunet allowed a leadoff single to Pagan. He would have faced Mays had San Francisco put one more runner on base. But the Braves' seventh pitcher of the day wisely retired the next three to strand the slugger in the on-deck circle, to the crowd's dismay.

"I probably was the only player who ever got booed on the road for making the last out," Davenport said with a laugh.

Beating up Milwaukee by a final of 14-4, the Giants vaulted to first place in the National League. San Francisco broke a league record by bashing 13 home runs in two days, and Mays tripled his 1961 home run total to date and raised his batting average 42 points to .333. So much for talk of a slump.

"How about some more ribs?" McCovey asked him back in the dugout. Sure enough, a smiling and laughing Mays fixed himself a plate of spare ribs and munched on them in the clubhouse.

"Man, you just don't hit like that every day," Mays told the writers. "This is the greatest day of my career."

The Game of My Life
By Willie Mays

It was those ribs the night before. I may have eaten too many or they may have been bad, I don't know. I was sick and throwing up. The next morning I couldn't stand. When I went to the ballpark, I wasn't feeling good. I wasn't going to play.

I took batting practice and a kid named Joe Amalfitano said, "Hey, try this bat. You might hit it good." Joey gave me the bat, and everything I hit went into the stands. I went over and changed the lineup. I put my name on it. Alvin saw it and he let it stay that way. I felt weak but I hit everything strong. Don't ask me how I did it.

What a thrill I had rounding the bases. The fans were great, even though it was Milwaukee. As I touched every base, they cheered. Here I was, not even expecting to play and now becoming a part of baseball history. I would have liked to come up in the ninth to see what I could do.

	1	2	3	4	5	6	7	8	9	R	H	E
Giants	1	0	3	3	0	4	0	3	0	14	14	0
Braves	3	0	0	0	0	1	0	0	0	4	8	1

Mays: 5 at-bats, 4 runs, 4 hits, 4 HR, 8 RBIs

In the clubhouse forty-five years later, Mays is still the center of the Giants universe. Current players, members of the team's staff, and his personal assistants orbit him like planets around a sun. Say Hey occupies his usual seat in the office of clubhouse manager Mike Murphy.

He still eats ribs "all the time," but they aren't on the menu on this evening. Instead, a locker room staffer fetches him a plate of nachos and a barbequed beef sandwich. After more than half a century of interviews, he's not thrilled to do another, though he does anyway. Today he's in a good mood.

"If I hit four home runs and we lost, it would have meant nothing to me. Instead, four homers and a win made it a happy clubhouse," Mays says.

"They were the five best swings you've ever seen," says Lon Simmons, the team's Hall of Fame broadcaster, joining the conversation. "Two of them didn't just clear the fence, they went out of the ballpark."

Mays has a lifetime Giants contract, with the title of "assistant to the president." He admits there's not much official work in the role. "I don't have a role," Mays said. "I come here and be me. I can't be anybody else. If I try to be someone else, I'm in trouble."

He is a frequent sight behind the scenes of the ballpark at 24 Willie Mays Plaza. The Hall of Famer appears on the field occasionally, too, for landmark homers of his godson Barry Bonds or special events like his 75th birthday in 2006. And his image is everywhere, from the statue outside the park's main entrance to photos throughout the stadium.

"That's a tribute, which I think is great," Mays said. "When they do that, it means they like you."

Armando Benitez leans into the room and waves. The Giants closer is in an agonizing slump; his blown saves contributed to a nine-game losing streak, and manager Felipe Alou has started to pull him from crucial situations when he falters. San Francisco fans are venting their frustration by booing him at every opportunity. Benitez can't even warm up in his home park without abuse from the crowd.

Mays stares at him for a moment. Then he grimaces as if in pain.

"Man, you're killing me," Mays tells the pitcher.

Benitez stiffens, though keeps his face straight and his mouth shut in front of the writers in the room. "I'm not saying nothing," the closer says. Mays' comment was not what Benitez wanted to hear, but he waits a minute more, hoping for a word of absolution from the team's patriarch, like innumerable Giants before him. Finally, Mays gives it to him. "You're going to be fine, just relax," he says.

Smiling, the pitcher turns to go. There's plenty of pain left in the season for Benitez, though tonight he'll pitch a perfect ninth inning for one of the only times all year.

Mays returns to his dinner and the interview, apparently unaware that he's just contradicted his statement about his function with the Giants. Despite the aging star's denials, Willie Mays still has a role in San Francisco, and he's just fulfilled it yet again.

3

FELIPE ALOU

"THE GOOD LORD HEARD MY PRAYER"

POSITION: right field

SEASONS WITH GIANTS: 1958–1963 as a player; 2003–2006 as a manager

ACCOMPLISHMENTS: All-Star in 1962, 1966 and 1968; led the Giants in batting average (.316) in 1962; led the National League in hits (218) and runs (122) in 1966; led Giants to 2003 National League West championship

GAME OF HIS LIFE: October 3, 1962 versus Los Angeles Dodgers

IN HIS LIFETIME OF baseball, Felipe Alou played in 2,082 major league contests and managed more than 2,000 more. His games in high school, college, the minor leagues, winter ball, and spring training account for at least another thousand. Only once, though, has the devout Christian prayed for his team to win a game.

That occurred on October 3, 1962, when the National League pennant race came down to a single game between the Giants and the Dodgers and a ninth-inning comeback for the ages.

"That ninth inning was the most electricity I ever felt in any particular baseball game or sport," said Alou.

For Alou, the 1962 season was significant for many reasons. The 27-year-old native of the Dominican Republic had come a long way from the fishing

19

village of Haina where he and his brothers grew up in poverty, swinging bats that their father hand-carved for them as they learned baseball. In his fifth year of big league ball, the Giants outfielder set career highs with his .316 batting average, 25 home runs, and 98 RBIs. He also made his first All-Star team.

"I think that had to be my best season," Alou said. "That was the year when I felt I established myself as a good player."

The Giants, however, appeared to be headed for a disappointing finish. The 1962 club boasted five future Hall of Famers including Willie Mays, Willie McCovey, Orlando Cepeda, Juan Marichal, and Gaylord Perry. Yet after closely trailing Los Angeles for much of the season, San Francisco fell back in the standings by four games after a six-game skid in late September. With only 11 games left to play, many players were close to giving up, Alou said.

At a team meeting in St. Louis, manager Alvin Dark told the players they still had time to win it and scheduled morning workouts for the duration of the season.

"We weren't executing. There were a lot of plays we just weren't making," Alou said. "We started winning games and then we really took the message seriously, started executing and playing really well."

The Giants' hot streak combined with the Dodgers' stumbling finish brought the teams into a tie on the last day of the regular season. In the years before divisional play, league rules called for a three-game tiebreaker series to determine a champion. Before the series even started, the pennant race drew comparisons to the epic battle of 1951, when the New York Giants came back from 13 games behind to tie the Brooklyn Dodgers. Bobby Thomson's "Shot Heard 'Round the World" in the ninth inning of the final game had won that tiebreaker series for the Giants.

This time, the series began at Candlestick Park, where Alou doubled in the first and scored on a Mays home run. Cepeda and third baseman Jim Davenport would homer too, and Giants ace Billy Pierce stifled the Dodgers

Felipe Alou's sharp eyes helped along the pennant-clinching rally on October 3, 1962. *Brace Photo*

in a 8-0 victory. The series then moved to Los Angeles, where fans were so disheartened by their team's collapse that only 25,321 attended the second game. The Giants jumped to 5-0 lead, but the Dodgers rallied in the sixth. Pinch hitter Lee Walls hit a bases-loaded triple to put the Dodgers ahead, 6-5, and first baseman Ron Fairly's sacrifice fly in the ninth finally won the roller-coaster contest for Los Angeles, 8-7.

The series was tied at a game apiece. A final contest in Los Angeles would determine the National League championship. San Francisco started Marichal in the finale against Dodgers southpaw Johnny Podres, who won 15 games for Los Angeles that year. Their hopes renewed by the home team's comeback, 45,693 fans attended the finale at Dodger Stadium.

The Giants took first blood against Podres in the third inning. Shortstop Jose Pagan singled, and Marichal tried to bunt him to second. Then, in what became a recurring theme of the game, the Dodgers contributed to their own demise through the first of four untimely errors. Podres botched the play, permitting Marichal to reach first and Pagan to advance to third. After Giants left fielder Harvey Kuenn singled to bring Pagan home, Podres had a chance to pick Marichal off second base. An errant throw allowed Marichal to advance to third and later score. Alou hit a single in the frame, and San Francisco took a 2-0 lead.

Podres and reliever Ed Roebuck would hold the Giants scoreless for the next five innings, while the Los Angeles bats began to make noise. Left fielder Duke Snider led off the fourth against Marichal with a double and soon scored. The Dodgers took a 3-2 lead in the sixth as Snider reached base again on a single, bringing up slugger Tommy Davis, who clubbed a two-run homer.

A San Francisco error led to a Dodger insurance run in the seventh, when speed demon Maury Wills singled and immediately stole second. After Wills broke for third, catcher Ed Bailey's wild throw allowed him to score. Los Angeles extended its lead to 4-2, but that wasn't the only thing about the play that bothered the Giants.

Leo Durocher, the Hall of Fame skipper who split 16 years managing the Brooklyn Dodgers and the New York Giants, served as Los Angeles' third base coach that year. After he waved Wills home on the error, Durocher broke for the plate as well in wild jubilation. The extraordinary sight of the third base coach tailing his base runner home—sliding in the dirt even as Wills slid across the plate—galled many Giants, including Alou. They may not have needed it, but Durocher's hot-dogging provided the Giants with added motivation.

After a scoreless eighth, San Francisco had one inning left to score at least two runs or else the Giants' long pennant drive would bitterly end. Due to hit fourth in the ninth, Alou stepped into the clubhouse between innings to pray: "God, I know you can help us win this game."

Roebuck had already pitched three innings, but Dodgers manager Walter Alston sent the weary reliever out for the ninth anyway, a decision that's been questioned ever since because of the talent available in the Los Angeles bullpen: Sandy Koufax, Don Drysdale, and Ron Perranoski.

"I was really beat," Roebuck later admitted. "It was the most uncomfortable I've ever felt in a game." But even after the disaster that would soon strike his club, Alston defended his decision: "I'd rather have Roebuck pitching for us with a two-run lead than anybody I've got," the skipper said.

Leading off the ninth was Felipe's younger brother, Matty Alou, a pinch hitter and part-time outfielder for the 1962 Giants, hitting in the pitcher's spot. He hammered Roebuck's second pitch into right for a single, and the historic rally began. Kuenn followed with a perfect double-play grounder to Wills at shortstop. But the Dodgers infield turned the play too slowly, forcing Matty Alou at second but failing to double up Kuenn.

Roebuck lost his command when McCovey came to the plate; the pitcher could not hit even the slugger's sizable strike zone. Representing the tying run, McCovey walked. That brought Felipe Alou to bat with runners on first and second. "My heart should have been thumping, but it wasn't, and I am sure it was because I had put my reliance on God instead of on myself," Alou recalled. With Mays on deck, the last thing Roebuck wanted to do was walk another batter to load the bases. But Alou worked the count full and finally took ball four.

Mays hit Roebuck's first pitch off the pitcher's hand. Had Roebuck picked it clean, he could easily have started a pennant-clinching double play. Instead, the ball squirted away from him, all the runners advanced safely, and a run scored.

"My heart was pounding as hard as ever and my stomach was flipping like a stricken flounder," Giants broadcaster Russ Hodges later wrote. "I had to take a tranquilizer to get through the ninth inning."

Now leading 4-3, Alston finally pulled Roebuck, only to make another questionable decision: he brought in neither of his future Hall of Famers, Koufax and Drysdale, but rather Stan Williams, a capable but unremarkable starter. It was as if the manager wanted to save his best pitchers for the World Series, many observers and critics later noted.

With the bases still loaded, Cepeda stepped in to face Williams. "It was one of the most important at-bats in my life," he recalled. "A pennant was on the line." After missing the first pitch, Cepeda lifted the second offering deep to right field. "I thought I might clear the bases, but Frank Howard made a great play. He was so tall that he reached up and caught it."

Nevertheless, the sacrifice fly tied the game, 4-4. It wouldn't stay tied for long. After the Dodgers walked Bailey intentionally to reload the bases, Davenport worked a walk to force Alou home from third. Back from the dead, the Giants took a 5-4 lead.

As the Dodgers sunk into deeper trouble by the minute, Alston turned to his bullpen again. At last Perranoski entered the game, and the ace reliever quickly induced a ground ball from Pagan to second base. However, the Los Angeles defense failed once more, as second baseman Larry Burright booted the ball. Another run scored. Pinch hitter Bob Nieman struck out to finally end the inning, but the Giants took a 6-4 lead to the bottom of the ninth.

Two days after his nine-inning shutout in Game 1, Pierce came in to pitch the bottom of the ninth. "This was going to be the pennant, so you're ready. Your arm could be falling off," Pierce said. "When you're going into a spot like that, you tell yourself you feel great whether it's true or not."

Pierce retired Wills on a ground ball to third. Then he induced third baseman Jim Gilliam to fly out to Mays in center field, and the Dodgers were down to their last out. As he had in Game 2, Alston summoned pinch hitter Walls, whose clutch triple the day before had given Los Angeles new life. There would be no such magic for the Dodgers this time. Walls lifted a fly ball to center. Mays put it away and then ecstatically hurled it into the center-field bleachers.

Eleven years later, the Giants had done it again, dramatically winning the pennant in an unbelievable comeback at the expense of their most detested opponents.

The Game of My Life
By Felipe Alou

That season was a great comeback, and that game was a great comeback. We arrived in the top of the ninth inning trailing, 4-2. I knew I was going to bat in that inning. As soon as the bottom of the eighth was over, I actually went to the clubhouse to pray and to ask God to help us. The prayer came because I couldn't believe that we came back from such a deficit only to (potentially) lose. That was going to be devastating to me and to the team.

Leo Durocher (the third base coach) ran all the way to home plate with Maury Wills. He was excited that he was doing it to us, to the Giants. It really hit me to see Durocher sliding next to Wills (as he scored in the seventh). I believe that's one of the reasons that led me to go to the clubhouse to pray so we could beat those guys.

There was so much pressure. There were so many opportunities to lose. We hit two balls that could have ended our chances. A groundball went right through the second baseman's legs, and Mays hit one right back to the pitcher. They had Ed Roebuck on the mound, one of the best fielding pitchers in the game at that time. He couldn't make a play. They couldn't make a play. It was incredible.

I can't believe how quiet that field was. That place was like a graveyard. The place was packed, but the fans didn't say anything. They were really, really dead through the entire inning.

I didn't do a whole lot in that game, but to me, my biggest thrill in baseball was when we won the game. I guess the good Lord heard my prayer, and that of thousands of people in the Bay Area.

	1	2	3	4	5	6	7	8	9	R	H	E
Giants	0	0	2	0	0	0	0	0	4	6	13	3
Dodgers	0	0	0	1	0	2	1	0	0	4	8	4

Alou: 4 at-bats, 1 run, 1 hit, 1 walk

———————

The ensuing celebration in the Giants clubhouse released the stress of not just that game, but the unrelenting pressure of the months-long chase. Cepeda, Marichal, and Pagan formed a conga line and danced enthusiastically for the television cameras. McCovey shouted into a microphone, "This is the greatest moment of my life!"

Among the horde of media and guests packed into Dodger Stadium's tiny visitors clubhouse was California gubernatorial candidate Richard Nixon, who told Dark, "Your players have heart."

Alou enjoyed a champagne shower and said a few words for the television cameras. Then he sought a quiet place to give thanks, finding a relatively calm spot in the shower room. "I went to bow down and thank God for the victory He had granted us," Alou recalled.

As thrilling as the victory was for the Giants, Alou couldn't help but sympathize with the Dodgers' excruciating pain. "I really felt bad for them, some of the nicer guys on the Dodgers like Ron Perranoski, Sandy Koufax, and Tommy Davis," he said. "I will always carry in my mind a picture of the Dodgers, heads bowed, faces sad, some with tears in their eyes, as they walked slowly to their clubhouse. . . . You wouldn't want your worst enemy to suffer that."

The scene in the Dodgers clubhouse was uglier than perhaps even Alou had imagined. The home team locked out the anxious press for an hour. A somber Snider emerged to ask the crowd of reporters for patience. The sounds of breaking glass and grown men crying escaped as he opened the door. "It's pretty grim in there," the left fielder told the writers.

That was made plain when the reporters finally entered the locker room. Littering the floor were broken beer bottles and the shredded remains of Dodgers uniforms which players had torn apart in anguish. Some Dodgers were so drunk they had passed out in the shower. Several of them openly derided Alston through his office's locked door. "Come on out here, you gutless son of a bitch!" cried one. "Tell us about your strategy, skipper. How we gonna play the World Series, you bastard?" Catcher John Roseboro was among those who left quickly. "I don't like to be around drunks," he explained. "It was the worst scene I ever saw with the Dodgers. It was one time we did not conduct ourselves with class."

For the Giants and their fans, though, the party was just beginning. The team flew back to a wild reception in San Francisco, starting at the airport, where as many as 50,000 people had overrun the fences and mobbed the runway. "They said inside the plane that we might have to land in Oakland," Alou said. "We had to circle for I don't know how long until they cleared the place." Most players' wives who came to meet their husbands at the airport never got within a mile of the place, and Alou was one of many Giants who had to hitch a ride home through the chaos.

Elsewhere in the city, pandemonium reigned. On Market Street, uncounted thousands honked horns, threw orange and black confetti from their windows, embraced strangers, shouted in joy, and drank. "There hasn't been anything like this since V-J Day," said one cabbie who witnessed the scene.

"Then we had to start the World Series the next day," Alou said. "There was not the same energy, not the same electricity. It was like we had won the World Series when we beat the Dodgers." In a series full of its own heroics and drama, the Yankees won in seven games.

Thousands of contests later, Alou has plenty of baseball memories to choose from. In his distinguished playing career, he once played the outfield with his brothers Matty and Jesus Alou, the only all-brothers outfield in major league history. As a manager, he returned to lead the club that signed him and has won more than 1,000 games, which is by far the most of any skipper born in Latin America. Yet the 1962 pennant-clinching game still tops Alou's highlights. Not only was it thrilling, it imparted a lesson that this baseball man has applied for decades.

"There's always a possibility of coming back," Alou said. "I often thought about that as a player, and also managing. I tell the guys, 'We have a chance,' right to the very end. There's always a shot."

4

BOBBY BOLIN

"DON'T LET THE BOOS BOTHER YOU"

POSITION: pitcher

SEASONS WITH GIANTS: 1961–1969

ACCOMPLISHMENTS: tied a major league record by striking out the first five batters in a game against the Dodgers in 1966; led Giants in shutouts (4) in 1966; set Giants single-season record in ERA (1.98) in 1968

GAME OF HIS LIFE: September 6, 1968 versus St. Louis Cardinals

---

BASEBALL HAS NO STATISTIC for booing, but Bobby Bolin figures St. Louis fans may own the league record. When he took the mound against the Cardinals on September 6, 1968, they filled Busch Stadium with boos so loud that he's still hearing the echoes.

"All I remember is the booing," Bolin said. "When I look back on individual games, that's the only one that stands out because I got booed so much."

The shy Giants pitcher nicknamed "B.B." was not even the type to inspire such hostility. The 29-year-old right-hander never showed up opponents, never argued with umpires, and was often overlooked on a San Francisco pitching staff that boasted future Hall of Famers Juan Marichal and Gaylord Perry.

But the fans who paid to see San Francisco play the Cardinals that day wanted a different game. The Giants had previously announced their ace

Marichal as starting pitcher, and the Cardinals countered with their great star Bob Gibson. The matchup of two dominant pitchers destined for Cooperstown thrilled the baseball-savvy St. Louis area. Then Giants manager Herman Franks changed his plan and decided to start Bolin instead. To maximize the team's chances to at least split the day's doubleheader, Franks decided Marichal would pitch the nightcap against southpaw Steve Carlton instead. (In hindsight, that wasn't a shabby matchup, either.)

"I'm not going to pitch Juan against Gibson," Franks told Bolin. "He might lose 1-0."

"What about me?" Bolin asked him. The manager laughed and walked away.

Angry Cardinals fans expressed their displeasure at Franks' bait-and-switch. Hot dog wrappers, peanuts bags, paper cups, and other trash rained on the field, accompanied by a long, thunderous round of boos.

"They'd come for miles, all over the Ozarks, to watch Gibson and Marichal pitch," Bolin said. "They had 48,000 people there that day. The papers and the radio were calling it the duel of the decade. Then here comes a guy named Bolin. They thought Bolin was made for the boos."

Despite Marichal's absence, the game unfolded as a pitching duel much as the crowd had expected. Gibson, strong and intimidating, utilized a blazing fastball, a tricky slider, and a big curve. He retired the Giants in order in the first with strikeouts of Bobby Bonds and Ron Hunt and a fly ball off the bat of Ty Cline.

The Cardinals lineup Bolin faced was a who's who of the era's stars and newsmakers. Leading off was the fleet-footed future Hall of Famer Lou Brock, followed by All-Star Curt Flood, who would later fight the baseball establishment to help bring free agency to the game. Then came slugger Roger Maris, the former Yankee who'd smashed 61 home runs to break Babe Ruth's cherished record. Batting cleanup was Orlando Cepeda, the former Giant and another future Hall of Famer who flourished in St. Louis.

In the game of his life, Bobby Bolin overcame a torrent of derision by St. Louis fans. *Brace Photo*

"Lou Brock stole a lot of bases so you had to get him out," Bolin said. "I would pitch him fastballs up and away and hope he popped them up. With Maris, you had to run the ball in on him quite a bit. Cepeda had that big heavy bat. He wore us out after we traded him to the Cardinals. I had to throw him a lot of sliders in the dirt. He could hit the ball hard, so I had to be careful not to throw him anything good."

Armed with this game plan, the hurler set to work. Bolin allowed a double to Maris in the first but retired the other Cardinals, and the inning ended with no score. San Francisco opened a promising second inning with singles by Willie McCovey and Jim Ray Hart, but Gibson crushed the rally by striking out Jesus Alou, Jack Hiatt, and Hal Lanier in succession.

Bolin answered back, retiring the Cards in order in the home half on three easy fly balls. A fresh round of abuse greeted B.B. when he came to bat in the third. Fans booed throughout the pitcher's at-bat, stopping and cheering only when their hero Gibson struck out Bolin.

In the next half-inning, Flood's RBI single gave St. Louis a 1-0 lead. But the Giants rallied back for two of their own in the fourth on two hits and a double by the catcher Hiatt. Frame after frame, Bolin made that lead hold up against the potent Cardinals offense. Bolin held the Cardinals hitless from the fourth through seventh innings as San Francisco tacked on a run in the sixth. When Bolin returned to the plate that frame for what turned out to be his last at-bat, he braced himself for more jeers and trash. But he discovered the fans' response to him had changed.

"After they tried everything in the world to beat me, they gave me a little clap," he said. "The Cardinals fans were never going to come over and be on my side, but they gave a little recognition to show they appreciated me."

The modest cheer gave the Giant a smile, though he still grounded out, going 0-3 on the day.

Bolin started the eighth inning and got two outs. After he allowed two singles and a run, the Giants skipper summoned reliever Frank Linzy, who retired four straight Cardinals to save the game.

Gibson won the Most Valuable Player and Cy Young Award in 1968, and his 1.12 ERA was baseball's best since 1913. But on September 6, Bolin was a run better, beating Gibson for the only time in his career.

The Game of My Life
By Bobby Bolin

Marichal was supposed to go against Gibson. The *St. Louis Post-Dispatch* called it the duel of the decade. People had bought tickets well in advance. When they saw I was pitching, they were really upset.

They threw everything on the field. I got a standing boo for five minutes. But Herman Franks was the one who spoiled their night. They should have been booing Herman and not me.

I knew there would be boos. The only thing I could do was say, "Golly, all this booing for me?" If people holler at you and boo you, it should boost how you play. I think it put a little spark in my pitching that night.

When I had a good slider going and my fastball, I could pitch a pretty good ballgame, and I usually pitched pretty good against the Cardinals. Gibson, when you pitch against him, you've got to have your best (stuff), because he's going to hang up some zeros.

What I learned from that game, and I talked about this around the country at seminars and motivational talks, is don't let the boos bother you. Don't let criticism or rejection bother you. Just keep on going and keep doing the right thing. People always remember what you do, and if you keep doing the right thing long enough, they'll remember the right things and good things you've done.

Then they might not come to your side, but at least they'll respect you.

	1	2	3	4	5	6	7	8	9	R	H	E
Giants	0	0	0	2	0	1	0	0	0	3	11	1
Cardinals	0	0	1	0	0	0	0	1	0	2	5	1

Bolin: win, 7⅓ innings pitched, 5 hits, 2 runs, 2 walks, 2 strikeouts

---

Bolin grew up playing ball with his brother on the family farm in rural South Carolina. He gained the attention of scouts by pitching five no-hitters in a row at the end of his high school career. He was plowing a mule in 1960 when Giants scout Tim Murchison drove out to meet him and nearly scared the mule to death with the noise of his loud Buick. "I figured that if anybody came that far looking for somebody to play ball, I ought to go ahead and play with him," the farmer-turned-pitcher said. Bolin signed the minor league contract for $4,000 and a bus ride to Florida.

When Bolin made the big club in 1961, "I was always in the middle," he said. "I was never classified as a starter or a reliever. I mostly sat on the tarp between the bullpen and the dugout because I didn't know whether I was going to relieve or start most of the time."

In fact, during Bolin's nine Giants seasons, he started 144 games and pitched out of the bullpen in 201 more. He won 73 against 56 losses and saved 21 games. In 1968, Bolin set a single-season Giants record for ERA at 1.98.

Bolin's star might have shown brighter in another time or place, but it was hard to wrest headlines away from the likes of Marichal and Perry. For instance, after Bolin's win against St. Louis, Marichal struggled to a win in the nightcap, 8-7. The ace gave up twice as many hits as Bolin and won his game on Willie Mays' bat and the strength of the Giants' defense and bullpen. But the banner headline in the next day's *San Francisco Chronicle* shouted, "Juan lurches to 25th in Giant Sweep," topping a story that focused on Marichal's pursuit of a 30-win season.

"That's the way life goes," Bolin said. "You don't really pay any attention to that. My highlight and biggest thrill was putting on a major league uniform. 'Here I am, a big league ballplayer.' Not many people could say that."

The Giants traded Bolin before the 1970 season, a decision he connects with his ballpark-bashing comments after a tough loss on July 5, 1969. San Francisco scored first that day and Bolin held Atlanta scoreless for four innings. Then the Candlestick wind kicked up strong enough to confound the Giants defense and blow away a hard-fought game.

The next day's papers carried the pitcher's sour stadium assessment: "They ought to pull the cork out of this thing and sink it right out there in the bay." Bolin's sentiment was hardly unique but reached the public the day before a city vote on a $9 million Candlestick improvement package. Management was not pleased.

"From that point on, it was all over," he said. Traded to the Milwaukee Brewers, Bolin also pitched for the Boston Red Sox before retiring after the 1973 campaign.

After baseball, he founded his own marketing company called Bolin Enterprises. "I travel all over the U.S., speak a lot, and they actually pay me for it," he said. A father and grandfather, Bolin settled in Easley, South Carolina, with his wife, Irene.

5

AL GALLAGHER

WHEN "DIRTY AL" CAME HOME

POSITION: third base

SEASONS WITH GIANTS: 1970–1973

ACCOMPLISHMENTS: first native San Francisco Giant; had ten game-winning RBIs in 1971

GAME OF HIS LIFE: June 28, 1970 versus Atlanta Braves

HE WASN'T A HALL OF FAMER, an All-Star, or even a standout as a major league player, though Al Gallagher became a favorite of Giants fans anyway.

Maybe his personality won their affection. The third baseman amused the crowds with backflips, handstands, and somersaults during infield practice. Unlike many teammates, he enjoyed signing autographs and chatting with the spectators.

His roots certainly didn't hurt. Gallagher enjoyed a singular distinction as the first San Francisco native to play for the Giants at Candlestick.

More than anything, though, fans loved his hard and hustling style of play. Diving for grounders or sliding into bases, "Dirty Al" never kept his uniform clean for long.

"When I got into the big leagues, they called me Dirty Al because I played hard, and after every play, I was dirty," Gallagher said. "I didn't mind diving in the dirt. That was the way I played the game."

Alan Mitchell Edward George Patrick Henry Gallagher—yes, he has five middle names—grew up in the city's Mission District. He was 12 years old in 1958 when the Giants arrived in San Francisco, but the young boy had followed baseball, and especially his favorite player Willie Mays, even before then.

"In those days you either rooted for Mickey Mantle or Willie Mays," Gallagher said. "Being a white guy, you'd think I'd be the Mantle type. But in 1957, Mickey Mantle came to San Francisco to play in an exhibition at Seals Stadium. I waited two and a half hours to get his autograph, and when he finally came out of the clubhouse, he pushed me. He was drunk.

"It was a very traumatic point in my life," he said. "I went home and took my Mantle rookie card—the one that's worth $25,000 today—and tore it up. So I was one of the few white guys who was a Mays fan. Then the Giants came to San Francisco in '58 and I got to see him play every day. What a thrill that was to me."

Gallagher grew up at the ballpark as much as a boy could, first at Seals, and later at Candlestick. He attended almost every home contest, sometimes scalping tickets and always fishing for batting practice baseballs that he could sell back for a dollar each. That would pay for a hot chocolate and his 90-cent ticket for the next game. When he didn't get a ball, Gallagher had a plan for that, also.

"Don't tell the police, but I used to sneak in," he said. "I'd jump over the fence. I went to about 70 games a year, as many home games as I could, except day games when I was in school."

Naturally, Gallagher became a player, too. "I didn't want to do anything else," he said. After his days at Mission High School, he played for Santa Clara University. There Dirty Al first picked up the nickname that followed him his entire career, thanks to his pledge not to wash his uniform during a long Broncos winning streak.

"I was very superstitious, and in our first game one year, I said that if I get a hit and we win the game, I'm not changing my uniform, including

38

Al Gallagher became the first San Francisco native to play for the Giants at Candlestick. *Brace Photo*

undergarments," Gallagher said. "Well, we won 24 in a row, and then lost the 25th of season, though I did get a hit in that game. By that time I had three empty lockers to each side. . . . Basically I got that moniker then, though I kept it up with different things that I did and the way I acted."

Indeed, it takes more than dirt to sum up Dirty Al. There were the wild antics, too, like the time he entered a greased pig contest, unwisely scheduled just before a college dance. "I caught the greased pig, threw it up in the air, and went to the microphone," he recalled. "And I made an announcement that the world's greatest greased pig catcher was Al Gallagher, in my typical manner. Then I went to the dance with this pig smell still all over me, smelling up high heaven."

Gallagher's high jinks would one day drive Giants manager Charlie Fox crazy, but they didn't prevent San Francisco from signing him in 1965. After five hard years in the minors, he reached the big club in 1970, fulfilling a dream to join his hometown team.

"My first major league game when I played on the same field as Willie Mays, Willie McCovey, and Bobby Bonds is a memory that means a lot to me," Gallagher said. "I was born and raised in San Francisco, and to me, these weren't just baseball players. They were my heroes."

The rookie's glove and rifle-like throwing arm won him starts at third base for most of the next two years. Gallagher and all the Giants had to adjust to Candlestick's brand-new AstroTurf. "It's a little faster than some of us thought," he said then, "but it can't be any harder than the Potrero Hill fields where I learned to play ball in San Francisco."

As a career .263 hitter, Gallagher didn't pummel the league with his bat, but he quickly developed a knack for timely hits. In his opening series against the Houston Astros, the Giant helped San Francisco win two out of three with six hits in his first 12 at-bats, knocking in the winning run in the second game. In 1971, Gallagher collected ten game-winning RBIs, eight alone in his sizzling month of August, to push the Giants toward an eventual division championship.

Gallagher hit just 11 home runs in his four big league seasons, few enough that he can remember them all, he jokes. But the most special was the one he crushed on June 28, 1970. In the first game of a doubleheader at Candlestick, the Giants and the Atlanta Braves duked it out in a back-and-forth, extra-inning fight. San Francisco led early on a McCovey home run in the second and a two-run double in the fourth by second baseman Bob Heise.

Juan Marichal held Atlanta scoreless on three hits in the first four innings, but the Braves began a comeback in the fifth when catcher Hal King tagged the Giants ace for a leadoff homer. Orlando Cepeda added a RBI single in the sixth, and Atlanta rallied for two runs on three singles in the seventh, taking a 4-3 lead. Bobby Bonds helped the Giants even the score with a leadoff double in the bottom half, later to score on a single by left fielder Ken Henderson. Then the bullpens took over, holding both clubs scoreless through the eighth and ninth innings.

Gallagher, then 24, turned some nice plays at third to retire Cepeda and Hank Aaron, but he had gotten nowhere all day against Atlanta's starter, Jim Nash, striking out, flying out, and grounding back to the pitcher twice in four at-bats. Dirty Al got another chance in the bottom of the tenth. McCovey and catcher Dick Dietz made quick outs, though Henderson singled again to bring up the third baseman. When Atlanta fireman Bob Priddy threw a fastball outside, Gallagher swung his bat murderously with every muscle in his 180-pound body. The ball flew so high and far that the Braves started trotting off the field before it touched down in the right-field bleachers.

Gallagher joyously rounded the bases behind Henderson on his way to a warm home-plate reception from his hero Mays and his other teammates. A standing crowd of 20,642 hollered its approval. The first home-grown San Francisco Giant had won the game and he didn't even have to get dirty to do it, though as usual his uniform was already soiled anyway.

The 6-4 winners enjoyed a brief celebration and prepared to go into battle again. The day was still young, and they had another game to play.

The Game of My Life
By Al Gallagher

I stunk it up before that home run. I struck out the first time. I didn't do very good off of Nash. I didn't think Nash threw it that good, but I didn't hit the ball. I was probably trying to take him back up the middle. That's what I usually did against sinker-slider pitchers.

Then in the tenth Priddy threw a fastball on the outside part of the plate, and I really hit that one good. That didn't happen very often. I never hit one that far before. I never hit a ball harder in my life. It was the first walk-off homer I ever had, and I never hit another one.

I got so excited. To win a game like that against a pretty good pitcher, wow. You don't get to do it too many times in your career. For a guy like me, that was it. Circling the bases was the fun part, with everyone yelling for me. That was my rookie season, and the fans were pretty excited. I was born and raised in San Francisco, and I was lucky enough to be a little bit of a fan favorite.

It was an exciting moment in my life, a wonderful feeling, to not only do something good myself but to help the team win.

	1	2	3	4	5	6	7	8	9	10	R	H	E
Braves	0	0	0	0	1	1	2	0	0	0	4	9	0
Giants	0	1	0	2	0	0	1	0	0	2	6	9	2

Gallagher: 5 at-bats, 1 run, 1, hit, 1 HR, 2RBIs

Gallagher cracked a single in the nightcap, which the Giants also won, 4-3. Another Giants hero of the day was 40-year-old pitcher Don McMahon, who won the first game and saved the second.

"Oh, that old fart, he was a great guy," Gallagher said of McMahon. "He was the oldest guy on the team, and he still threw harder than any of the young kids."

Gallagher admits that he was a bit goofy, but his teammates fortunately took care of him. A case in point was Dirty Al's fashion sense, or his lack thereof, which came up during an airborne kangaroo court session in his rookie year. Gallagher's plaid shirts, striped pants, and mismatched socks were brought to the attention of McCovey, the judge. Mays couldn't take it anymore, recalled pitcher Jim Barr.

"Mays gets up in the back of the plane," Barr said. "He says, 'I've got $100 I'm gonna donate for Al Gallagher if anybody will go out and buy him a pair of pants and socks and shirts that match!' Back then, $100 could buy a few things. Everybody started rolling."

Gallagher amused his teammates with his pranks too, like the time he slid into beat writer Bucky Walter in an airport waiting room. "I was just having a little fun with Bucky," he said. "I decided I would do a hook slide. I did catch him so he didn't fall and get hurt."

When Gallagher pulled a similar stunt on his skipper, though, he may have gone too far.

"Dirty Al, boy, he was crazy. You didn't know what he was gonna do next," said teammate Tito Fuentes. "We were at the airport, two hours before the flight, doing nothing, so we said to him, 'We'll give you money if you slide into Charlie Fox.' At first he said no, but we gave him $100, so he goes in running and slides head first into Charlie Fox's feet. We gave him the money, but Charlie Fox fined him, I don't know how much, for embarrassing the team."

The businesslike Fox became aggravated with his wild third baseman and reduced his playing time in 1972. San Francisco traded Gallagher to the California Angels in 1973, and his big league days ended after that season.

Gallagher taught sixth grade for nine years after his playing career, and he also stayed in baseball. Once the game's leading oddball, Dirty Al could have won a poll as the least likely player to join management, but he successfully led minor league clubs like the Durham Bulls, the Kansas City T-Bones and the St. Joseph Blacksnakes for more than 15 years and over 1,000 wins. "I love it." Gallagher said. "I've been fortunate enough to have had 29 guys reach the majors, and I get the thrill of seeing those guys in the major leagues.

"Baseball to me is still a lot of fun," he said. "I still get to be a kid. It's a good deal. Not too many guys get to live their dream for as long as I've been able to."

6

TITO FUENTES

"CRYING LIKE A BABY"

POSITION: second base

SEASONS WITH GIANTS: 1965–1974

ACCOMPLISHMENTS: led Giants in doubles (33) in 1972; set Giants single-season record for fielding percentage by a second baseman (.993) in 1973

GAME OF HIS LIFE: September 30, 1971 versus San Diego Padres

WHEN THE GAME ENDED, the Giants stormed off the field screaming triumphantly. Champagne soaked their clubhouse for the first time in nine years, and the room quickly filled with the sounds of laughter and celebration. San Francisco Mayor Joe Alioto, who made the trip to San Diego Stadium, congratulated the players one by one. Everyone wanted to shake hands with pitcher Juan Marichal, who stifled the Padres in a complete-game win.

"Man, this is tremendous. My greatest thrill. Nothing like it," Marichal said. "It was the biggest game of my life."

As bubbly sprayed the room, one of the few who actually downed any was Giants manager Charlie Fox. After an exhausting playoff race that lasted until the final game, no one questioned that he had earned a drink. "God, how those kids out there battled for this one," said the emotional skipper.

So merry was the gala that the players nearly overlooked one Giant who didn't join the party. But as soon as he ran into the room, Tito Fuentes fell to the floor face-down. His teammates drew around and tried to rouse him, but the second baseman would not move. Joyful shouting was replaced with sudden alarm.

"Doc, doc!" cried catcher Dick Dietz. "Tito's hurt!"

September 30, 1971, was a life-changing day for Fuentes, then 27 and a Giant for seven years. It was the last day of the regular season, and San Francisco had led the National League West all year. Stars of the 1960s like Willie Mays, Willie McCovey, and Marichal had lifted the team to an eight-game lead in August. But the club nearly collapsed in September, losing 15 of 21 before the last series against the Padres. In the final days, the Los Angeles Dodgers climbed within a single game.

On Wednesday, September 29, the struggling Giants had a chance to clinch the championship with a win against woeful San Diego. The low-scoring contest reached the tenth inning when the Padres mounted a rally. Fuentes got a chance to start an inning-ending double play when San Diego's Johnny Jeter hit a ground ball to second. But the second baseman dropped the ball and got no one out, bringing up the Padres' Nate Colbert, who belted a game-winning three-run homer.

Fuentes was miserable. "Although nobody said anything, I felt the boys thought I was the reason they lost," he said. "I would still play that ball the same way if I had to do it again. But I wouldn't drop it."

Actually, the players knew better than to pin the loss on one man, said teammate Jim Barr. "Tito put a lot of pressure on himself thinking that, but we knew it wasn't one guy's fault," said Barr, a rookie on the 1971 team. "We knew we had the ability to come back the next day."

Fortunately for the Giants, the Dodgers lost that night, too, so San Francisco remained a game ahead, still able to clinch the division with a win on Thursday. For a roster of aging stars making their last hurrah and hungry

Tito Fuentes cracked three hits and turned two double plays in the Giants' division-clinching game on September 30, 1971. *Brace Photo*

youngsters like Fuentes who had never reached the playoffs, the last game was a must-win. The Giants had no doubt that the Dodgers would prevail in their final contest, forcing a sudden-death tiebreaker if San Francisco should stumble.

September 30 held the promise of postseason fulfillment for the Giants and redemption for their second baseman, but for Fuentes, there would be something more. That morning he got news about his pregnant wife during breakfast at the team's San Diego hotel. She had delivered their sixth child, a boy, and the nurses at the Bay Area hospital called to talk about a name for the lad. "You can call him 'Clinch' if we win tonight," the father told them in all seriousness.

Last-place San Diego, losers of 99 games already, played according to baseball's code that even non-contenders must make every effort to win games with playoff implications. Starting for the Padres was their finest pitcher, Dave Roberts, winner of 14 games and runner-up in the league rankings with a 2.10 ERA.

Fuentes got things started quickly hitting a one-out double in the first, with a chance to score two batters later when McCovey roped a single to right. However, right fielder Ollie Brown fired a bullet home to nail Fuentes at the plate. It was the only scoring opportunity for either team until the fourth, when the second baseman came to bat again. Fuentes connected against Roberts once more, cracking a line-drive single to left. Mays followed with a double, and this time the hustling Fuentes scored all the way from first without a play.

Suffering from a muscle pull in his rib cage, Bobby Bonds had scratched himself from the lineup that night. Taking his place in right field was the young prospect Dave Kingman, a major leaguer for just two months. Kingman took a ball and a strike from the Padres ace, and then unloaded on a fastball for a two-run moon shot. The biggest hit of his young career put the Giants ahead, 3-0. The rookie thrust both fists in the air as he tore around the bases, finally to fall into the arms of an ecstatic Giants dugout.

"I got it a little on the hands," Kingman said. "I was too busy running to see it go out. I almost fell over when I saw the umpire give the sign. It's the greatest feeling in the world."

Throughout the game, San Francisco's future Hall of Famers played up to their names. Mays, then 40, ran like he had ten years earlier, stealing second and third in the fifth inning. McCovey struck for two hits and walked. And Marichal handcuffed the Padres all night long.

San Diego managed just one hit against the Dominican Dandy in the first four frames. Then the Padres rallied in the fifth when Brown reached on an error. The right fielder hit a ground ball far to the left of Fuentes, which the second baseman snared in a dazzling play. He threw to first in time, but Marichal dropped the ball. The pitcher furiously pounded his glove in aggravation. "Keep your cool, man," Fuentes told his teammate. Brown advanced to second on a ground ball, and then scored on a single by catcher Bob Barton. San Diego's Tommy Dean came to bat as the potential tying run, but Marichal got a timely lift from his defense. Dean hit a ground ball in the hole that shortstop Chris Speier chased down and turned into a 6-4-3 double play.

In the seventh inning, the Padres brought in pitcher Mike Corkins. Once a Giants minor leaguer, Corkins made his way into the baseball history books with two unique distinctions. He served up Mays' 600th home run in 1969, and he once hit the same batter three times in a game, a record. That batter was none other than Fuentes, who was remarkably forgiving about it.

"That became a *Jeopardy* question," Fuentes said. "He threw hard and he was wild. I liked the guy and didn't want to charge him. Besides, he was a big son of a bitch. I'm glad I got a hit off him."

Fuentes singled against Corkins for his third hit of the night, though the inning ended with him marooned at first. After seven innings, the Giants maintained a 3-1 lead.

In the San Diego eighth, Barton led off with another single, bringing up the shortstop Dean. Once again, the Padre hit a grounder to Speier, who threw to second. Fuentes made the pivot and threw to first. The double play was a carbon copy of the first twin killing, right down to the players involved on both teams. Following his costly bungle in the previous game, Fuentes was delighted.

"I didn't want to make a mistake," the second baseman said. "I was really determined to do it after the day before."

San Francisco added insurance in the ninth when Speier doubled and scored on another two-bagger by left fielder Ken Henderson. Fuentes advanced Henderson to third with a fly ball. That became significant because San Diego pitcher Al Severinsen committed a balk, allowing the run to score and the Giants' lead to increase to 5-1.

The extra runs were comforting because around this time, the San Diego scoreboard flashed a final score from Los Angeles. The Dodgers had defeated the Houston Astros, 2-1, to climb within a half-game of first place. San Francisco had to hang on to win the division. Three outs separated the team from a championship.

Marichal pitched the game despite a sore hip, injured in an on-field collision in Cincinnati, which prevented him from making his usual delivery. "The hip hurt," he said. "I couldn't kick as high as usual. But maybe it helped my control. I had a good fastball." Marichal would throw only 81 pitches in the game, 69 of them strikes.

In the bottom of the ninth, Marichal surrendered a double to third baseman Garry Jestadt, but got two outs on two fly balls. Then Colbert, the Padres' hero of the previous game, hit a ground ball to short. So excited was Fuentes that he raced to embrace Marichal on the mound before Speier threw the ball to first. The second baseman ran into the line of fire in his enthusiasm; the ball missed his head by a whisker.

Finished at last was the dog-eat-dog playoff race. San Francisco had won the National League West for the first time, three years after divisional play began in 1969. Some Giants fans in attendance among the 34,861 in San Diego Stadium cheered for the new champions. Many Padres fans had already left, and the remaining partisans swallowed their team's 100th loss with quiet resignation.

Relief, joy, and exhilaration welled up in Fuentes as he joined the orange and black stampede. Once inside the clubhouse door, his emotions overwhelmed him and he broke into sobs before tumbling to the floor. To hide his tears, an embarrassed Fuentes laid face down as his mates surrounded him in concern.

Finally, Gaylord Perry lifted him up and diagnosed his condition for the assembled crowd. "He's crying like a baby," the pitcher shouted with a laugh. "Pour the champagne!" The party resumed as Fuentes climbed to his feet.

"They tried to turn me over, but I was refusing because I was crying and I didn't want anyone to see me," Fuentes recalled. "And when they finally turned me over and saw that I was happy, they started screaming again." The most emotional Giant of them all congratulated each of his teammates, sobbing anew with each embrace.

The Game of My Life
By Tito Fuentes

We lost a game on Saturday (Wednesday) and I've always believed I contributed to that loss. I felt bad, but those things happen—what can you do? That forced us to start Marichal. We wanted [to save] him for the first game of the playoffs, but if we didn't pitch Marichal and we lost, then we would be in a tiebreaker and you never know what's going to happen in one day.

We jumped on Roberts. He threw a screwball and knew how to keep the ball down low. You wait and wait and think it's a good pitch and then [it] falls to the ground. I don't think I owned him, but I hit him on that day. I got a double right away, so at least I was contributing. I went on to score and we never relinquished the lead.

After the last ground ball, I started running to the pitcher. Speier threw to McCovey and he almost hit me. I just wanted to go to the mound and hug Marichal and the ball just missed. That could have been a disaster. If it would have hit me, the guy gets on first base and I don't know what would have happened.

Later, I got champagne poured on my head and I was still crying, crying in relief because we had won.

	1	2	3	4	5	6	7	8	9	R	H	E
Giants	0	0	0	3	0	0	0	0	2	5	10	1
Padres	0	0	0	0	1	0	0	0	0	1	5	0

Fuentes: 5 at-bats, 1 run, 3 hits, 1 double, turned 2 double plays

---

A day's rest before the playoffs began enabled the Giants to fully celebrate their achievement, both before and after they flew back to the Bay Area. Fuentes enjoyed himself so much that he woke up in a strange house the next morning.

"We partied all night," Fuentes said. "When I woke up the next day, I looked around and didn't know where I was. 'How in the hell did I get here? Don't ask me!' So then of course I took a taxi and went home." His next stop was the hospital room of his wife and newborn son, where he "played down" the events of his previous evening.

Clinch Fuentes attended UCLA on a scholarship and became a biologist. If he was ever dismayed by the curious name his parents chose for him, he could at least be grateful that they didn't choose one even more unusual. The couple considered naming the youngster "W.S.," for World Series, Fuentes said. Considering the results of the playoffs, it's probably best that they didn't.

San Francisco won its first game of the best-of-five National League Championship Series, beating Pittsburgh, 5-4. Perry threw a complete game, and Fuentes contributed a two-run homer. But the Pirates won the next three and the National League pennant on their way to a World Series championship over the Baltimore Orioles.

Nevertheless, the 1971 Giants took great pride in winning a division championship with a roster that didn't compare well on paper with San Francisco teams of the 1960s.

"Mays was on the way down and didn't have a good year," Fuentes said. "McCovey was a little hurt. We did not have one guy hitting .300, but we won by a combination of everyone doing the little things. All 25 guys did something to contribute to the victory."

The teamwork led to strong camaraderie, Fuentes said. "We had great, great fun. We'd go to the sauna after the game in the ballpark and drink beer and talk about what the next day was to be, and we had so much confidence because we never lost first place," the Giant recalled. "That was the only year I can really remember the players feeling for each other on and off the field."

Fuentes fled his native Cuba at 18 years old to join the Giants organization in 1962. He reached the big club in 1965, and started at second base for most of the next nine seasons. His flashy style of play both endeared him to his mates and motivated rival pitchers to occasionally bean him. Fuentes liked to give his bat a no-look bounce off the plate before each at-bat and needle opposing base runners who came within earshot of his spot on the infield.

"If you played with Tito Fuentes, you loved him, and if you played against him, you hated him," said teammate Al Gallagher. "He had a flamboyant hot dog streak, but he didn't do that to show off or for all the reasons that you thought. He was just having fun."

Fuentes settled in Reno, Nevada, with his wife, Elvia, and stays active in the Giants organization. He participates in the team's fantasy camps and promotional events. Most of all, he broadcasts Giants and other baseball games for Spanish television and radio stations. Fuentes enjoys this role because it keeps him close to the game, and for another reason, too.

"I get paid for something that I like to do, which is talk," he said.

7

GREG MINTON

PAYBACK

POSITION: pitcher

SEASONS WITH GIANTS: 1975–1987

ACCOMPLISHMENTS: All-Star in 1982; set Giants single-season record in saves (30) in 1982; set major league record for pitching 269 1/3 consecutive innings without allowing a home run

GAME OF HIS LIFE: October 3, 1982 versus Los Angeles Dodgers

WHEN JOE MORGAN HIT one of most fabled home runs in the rivalry and Tommy Lasorda shook his head and covered his grief-stricken face, 47,457 of the most bloodthirsty fans to ever see a game at Candlestick Park reveled in a sadistic celebration. The Giants-Dodgers contest of October 3, 1982 became San Francisco's timeless monument to payback and revenge. No one enjoyed it more than Greg Minton, the off-beat Giants closer whose dislike of boys in blue ran deep.

"I grew up in Solana Beach in the '60s, protesting anything and everything," Minton said. "We were supposed to like the Dodgers, the closest major league team to us. The last thing I was going to do was like the team I was supposed to like. So the Dodgers and I always had a non-love affair."

That sentiment only deepened in Minton's first seven seasons with San Francisco. In those years, the Giants placed no higher than third in the National League West and finished with losing records five times. To make things worse, Los Angeles topped the orange and black in each of those campaigns. Dodger skipper Tommy Lasorda became famous in those years for taunting San Francisco fans, blowing them kisses when his club visited Candlestick.

"In my first few years on the Giants, we got our ass kicked by those guys just about every time. Finally, we got a competitive team in '82. We put on a real good run and got a serious adrenaline flow working," Minton said. "I simply can't explain that feeling, the high I would get every day. Every game somebody would do something that was ordinarily impossible."

San Francisco won 20 of 27 games that magical September, including a three-game sweep of their rivals in Los Angeles. Entering the final weekend at Candlestick Park, the Giants and Dodgers were tied in the National League West standings, both one game back of the first-place Braves. Los Angeles won the Friday night series opener, 4-0, on Jerry Reuss' complete game and Rick Monday's grand slam. Then on Saturday, the Dodgers routed the Giants, 15-2, to eliminate San Francisco from the playoff race.

Only one purpose remained for the Giants in Sunday's finale: to avenge themselves on Los Angeles, which was still one game out of first. That opportunity proved to be a powerful motivation for San Francisco on the last day of the regular season. Manager Frank Robinson started his best available lineup, including Morgan, a future Hall of Famer, and Bill Laskey, the team's best starting pitcher. Lasorda sent to the mound his ace and All-Star, Fernando Valenzuela.

Dodgers third baseman Ron Cey hit a two-run homer in the second. The Giants answered right back in the home half, scoring on Johnnie LeMaster's bases-loaded walk and again on a no-out double play. Otherwise, Laskey and Valenzuela kept their respective opponents' bats quiet. After the first six innings, the score was 2-2.

With one out in the seventh, Monday and Cey hit consecutive singles off Laskey. Robinson sent for southpaw Gary Lavelle to face Jose Morales, only to see the pinch hitter beat out an infield hit to second. Once again

Greg Minton escaped trouble in the seventh to help eliminate the Dodgers from the 1982 playoffs. *SF Giants*

the skipper called the bullpen, summoning Minton, 31, to wiggle out of a bases-loaded jam.

"Moonie" had the best season of his life in 1982, though he'd already pitched 120 innings, the most in his career so far. The closer also finished more games than any pitcher in the National League that year. Fatigued but "pumped" to help eliminate Los Angeles, Minton relied almost entirely on his low-90s fastball. It was enough. First, the Giant struck out Bill Russell, and then he induced Jorge Orta to ground out to second. San Francisco escaped with the game still tied.

"That was the turning point," recalled Laskey. "When Moonie stopped them there, I figured we had 'em."

After the game, the Dodgers looked back on this frame with painful regret for another reason that wasn't evident to the spectators. Lasorda had sent Orta to pinch-hit for Valenzuela because he believed the pitcher had developed an arm problem. Later, the Dodgers determined that this wasn't true, that Valenzuela was tiring but was still able to continue. Their faulty communication with their Spanish-speaking star cost them dearly, because it set up a fatal confrontation in the Giants' seventh.

Tom Niedenfuer took the mound for Los Angeles, and Bob Brenly greeted him with a leadoff single. Then Champ Summers ripped a double, bringing up San Francisco's closer. Minton batted .176 in 1982, not bad for a relief pitcher, though Niedenfuer got him swinging for the first out of the inning. Lasorda then called in southpaw Terry Forster, who fanned Jim Wohlford for the second out. For a moment, it seemed the Dodgers would escape their jam, just as the Giants had moments before. But first, Forster had to face the left-handed hitting Morgan, who stepped in for his greatest San Francisco moment.

Forster got ahead, 1-2, but on his fourth pitch he hung a slider, and Morgan drilled it over the right-field fence for a three-run homer. The second baseman circled the bases with his right arm raised in triumph as the ravenous crowd went wild. With his hands on his hips, an exasperated Forster watched the ball fly out and furiously threw his glove in the air.

"I got my A-No. 1 good swing at it, and when I hit them that good, they usually go out," Morgan said.

Leading 5-2, the Giants still needed six outs to complete their retribution. Robinson trusted only Minton to get each one of them. First, the pitcher jammed Steve Sax, who grounded out to second. Then the Dodgers' Ken Landreaux and Dusty Baker hit back-to-back doubles to score a run and threaten for more.

"I had real good success against Dusty early in my career, and then I met the man," Minton said. "He said, 'God dang it, Moonie, I can't hit that slider of yours no matter what.' Later I realized every pitch he'd ever hit off me was a slider. I've got to give it to Dusty, he did a heck of a job setting me up, and he hit me way better later in my career."

Next up was Steve Garvey, a noted Giant-killer. Still throwing only fastballs, Minton worked the count to 2-2. The savvy catcher Brenly, who had eyed Baker signaling pitch location to the batter from second base, trotted to the mound for a private word with his pitcher. Seconds later, Garvey struck out looking at Minton's outside heater.

"Baker was pointing to his left shoulder for inside and his right shoulder for outside, and Bobby caught him doing it," Minton said. "He came out and told me to go away from where he set his target up. So on 2-2 he set up inside and I put a fastball right on the (outside). I felt sorry for Garvey. He was crossed up."

Back for the eighth, Forster retired San Francisco's Reggie Smith, Darrell Evans, and Jeffrey Leonard in order. So Minton got a scant breather before returning for his third inning of work with a 5-3 lead. By this time, the scoreboard showed that Atlanta had lost in San Diego. Los Angeles could join the Braves in first place and force a tiebreaker with a win. Yet the Dodgers could do nothing with the Giants' All-Star closer. In the ninth, Cey grounded out to third, and Minton struck out pinch hitter Ron Roenicke.

As Los Angeles' moment of elimination grew near, the crowd's bloodlust grew ever stronger. "I don't brake for Dodgers" read the sign of one rabid fan. All in the stadium were on their feet. When Moonie got Russell to ground to third to end the ballgame, the raucous fans screamed in ecstasy, demanding a victory lap from their Giants. Minton, the winning pitcher, and his teammates enjoyed their encore as the Candlestick sound system played Tony Bennett's "I left my heart in San Francisco."

In the visitors' clubhouse, the Dodgers agonized. A stunned Lasorda fought back tears.

"It was the worst exhibition in my career," moaned Forster. "What alias can I go under?" His teammates tried to comfort him, with little success.

"Remembrances of a season can be cruel," Monday said. "You remember it by one pitch, instead of the hundreds Terry threw that allowed us to get this far."

To the Giants, though, the game marked a significant improvement from the outcome of previous years. While Atlanta won the division, San Francisco made that result possible by playing Los Angeles tough.

"This has to be the most exciting year since I bought the team in '76. The team really played beautifully," said owner Bob Lurie.

"I thought it was a very important game for the team, for the organization, and for the season. The Dodgers have manhandled this club for the last four or five years. . . . We wound up knocking them out at the end," said Robinson.

"I don't know if there's such a thing as a next-best thing," said the skipper, "but if there is, this was it."

The Game of My Life
By Greg Minton

With two days left, it's the Braves, Dodgers, and Giants. For those of us who weren't even all-league players in high school, holy shit, we are pumped.

Anyway, the Dodgers knock us out with one day to go, and it's them and Atlanta still fighting for first. In the seventh inning, they get it going and we say, "Oh shit, the Dodgers are going to win this thing again." So I get called in the seventh to try to get us out of the jam.

I loved those situations with the bases loaded or two on and two out. If you're a quality reliever, that's the exact reason you come to the ballpark. That's the sole reason you want to be a closer, to face those moments in that role. Your focus is better, your thinking is clearer. Those are the greatest times.

I had never experienced anything like the crowd's reaction after that game. Our whole team got a curtain call. The Dodgers are going through the tunnel, and we're tipping our hats on the field. I don't know them, I never met them, but they're giving us a standing ovation. They appreciated us that much. They were happy as heck that we finally beat the Dodgers. It was great that what we had done was fulfilling for them too.

We found out later the Braves were watching the game in their locker room. I was the most popular guy in Atlanta for three hours. That was huge for the Giants to finally have an opportunity to do something to the Dodgers, instead of the other way around. It felt a little sweeter than probably any of us had expected. I spent my whole life not liking the Dodgers, so playing for the Giants and knocking them out made it a big moment.

	1	2	3	4	5	6	7	8	9	R	H	E
Dodgers	0	2	0	0	0	0	0	1	0	3	9	0
Giants	0	2	0	0	0	0	3	0	X	5	5	0

Minton: win, 2⅔ innings pitched, 2 hits, 1 run, 0 walks, 3 strikeouts

---

During his 13 years pitching for San Francisco, the friendly Minton was known for his devastating sinker and eccentric personality. His best pitch enabled him to break his team's single-season record with 30 saves and shatter a major league record with 269 1/3 consecutive innings without allowing a home run.

"Minton was tough. I didn't like facing him," Baker recalled. "He bore that heavy sinker in on you, and he threw sliders away. He always kept you conscious of that sinker in on your hands."

His personality? Minton's teammates didn't call him Moonie for nothing. Whether he was blasting Pink Floyd in the shower room, or highjacking the team bus for kicks, or buzzing his manager with a hang glider, the pitcher always seemed a little bit "spacey" to his fellow players.

"I cultivated that flaky reputation, because if batters think you might be just a little insane, you've got a jump on them," the Giant explained.

Minton has coached and managed in the minor leagues, and worked for a Livermore swimming pool refurbishing company. A father and grandfather, he recently moved to Danville, California.

Successive closers have broken Minton's team saves record, though San Francisco's video operators never tire of replaying his best game's highlights on giant ballpark screens. It's a favorite of longtime Giants fans who remember when the guilty pleasures of payback and revenge were all they or their team had.

Whatever private satisfaction San Francisco's players took from exterminating their foes in 1982, the Giants avoided public gloating about the Dodgers' demise.

"I have sympathy for those guys," Morgan said that day. "It's tough to be over there with your head down because you needed to win the last game and couldn't do it." His home run was "for the Giants and not to the Dodgers," the second baseman said.

Minton, too, keeps mum about the contest when he meets old Dodgers at golf tournaments and the like, even if he flashes them a knowing "we got you" grin.

"It would be very unclassy to say to them, 'Remember the time . . . ?'" Minton said. "We just don't do that. But you don't have to bring it up. Everybody remembers that game."

8

DAN GLADDEN

MARVEL IN THE MUCK

POSITION: center field

SEASONS WITH GIANTS: 1983–1986

ACCOMPLISHMENTS: set San Francisco Giants rookie single-season record for stolen bases (31) in 1984; led Giants in runs (64), stolen bases (32), and triples (8) in 1985

GAME OF HIS LIFE: April 26, 1985 versus Cincinnati Reds

SAN FRANCISCO ENJOYED A dreamy comeback one day in 1985, though it's an easy game to overlook from an otherwise nightmarish season. The Giants' woeful 100 losses buried the early gem like enough manure to fill up Candlestick Park. "I don't recall that one," said broadcaster Hank Greenwald. "I didn't think we won any games that year."

For most of the evening, the April 26 contest looked like another one best erased from memory to the Giants and their fans. Before it ended, however, the team's improbable rally became the favorite San Francisco memory of center fielder Dan Gladden.

Cincinnati roughed up Giants starter Atlee Hammaker, starting with Reds shortstop Dave Concepcion, who homered to left in the second. Then back-to-back doubles started a Cincinnati rally in the fourth. Before the Giants knew it, the Reds had jumped ahead, 4-0.

Cincinnati starter Jay Tibbs opened the game with three perfect frames, but Gladden helped San Francisco get a run back in the bottom of the fourth. The center fielder led off with a sharp single to center, and second baseman Manny Trillo followed with another hit. Right fielder Chili Davis advanced both runners with a slow roller to second, and left fielder Jeffrey Leonard scored Gladden with a ground out.

Hammaker got two quick outs in the top of the fifth before Cesar Cedeno doubled and Nick Esasky smacked a two-run homer to center. The Reds rally sent the southpaw to the showers and reclaimed the momentum for Cincinnati, leading 6-1.

"I ran out of gas a little in the fourth inning," said Hammaker. "I struck out seven so I must have had something early, but after the fourth I was getting everything up and couldn't fool anybody."

For the rest of the way, the Giants bullpen pitched marvelously. Greg Minton, Frank Williams, and Vida Blue combined for four shutout frames. Their effort appeared to be in vain, though, because Tibbs continued to silence San Francisco's bats. The Giants managed only two more hits through the eighth, and few of the 12,534 paying customers stayed for what promised to be a dreary conclusion.

Then San Francisco's fortunes changed wildly in the bottom of the ninth, starting with Davis' fly ball double down the left field line. Leonard singled to center, scoring Davis and bringing up first baseman Scot Thompson, who delivered another base hit. Concerned but still leading by 6-2, Reds manager Pete Rose called in Ted Power from the Cincinnati bullpen. The hard-throwing righty saved a career-high 27 games in 1985, though the April 26 contest was not among his highlights. Power got catcher Bob Brenly to ground to the shortstop for the first out, as Thompson and Leonard advanced to second and third. Next was third baseman Brad Wellman, who blooped a hit to left to knock both base runners home and bring the Giants within two runs.

"I thought I was going to get a hit," Wellman said. "It was a chip shot off the end of the bat, but I was able to put it out there."

Dan Gladden usually chocked up on the bat, but on April 26, 1985, he swung for the fences against the Reds. *Brace Photo*

Power induced pinch hitter Joel Youngblood to hit a ground ball for the second out, but he made a critical mistake against utility player David Green. On four pitches, the closer walked the pinch hitter batting just .069 to that point in 1985. That finally got the crowd excited because the possible winning run came to the plate.

The batter was Gladden, then 27 and playing in his first full big league season. A Bay Area native who had attended Cal State Fresno, the Giant was already known for his intensity and hustling style of play. "I was somebody who played like it was his last game every day," Gladden said. In fact, the center fielder often dirtied his uniforms stealing bases, diving for catches in the outfield, and occasionally in brawls.

"I don't remember a game he ever played when he didn't stick his nose in the dirt and give 101 percent," said Minton.

Throughout his career, Gladden's best success came as a contact hitter; true to form, he hadn't hit a home run yet in 1985. But when Power's first two pitches drifted out of the strike zone, Gladden figured he and his last-place club had nothing to lose. Instead of choking up on the bat for a base-hit swing, the leadoff hitter lowered his hands and swung from his heels.

"It took me a year to convince Danny to choke up and go for contact, not home runs," said San Francisco hitting coach Tom McCraw. "But when he dropped down to the end of the bat, I knew what he was going to do."

Gladden drilled Power's heater high and deep, and the ball easily cleared the left-field fence. The three-run homer capped the Giants' biggest comeback of the year. Despite trailing by five runs in the ninth, San Francisco had won the ballgame, 7-6. The Giants and their few remaining fans jumped out of their seats and howled.

"I almost hit my head on the top of the dugout," said Thompson.

"I kept on crouching low so I could lower that outfield fence and make it easier for the ball to go out," said Brenly.

Rookie manager Jim Davenport lost his job before the season ended, but the skipper was all smiles after Gladden's walk-off blast. "That was about as good a comeback as I've seen," he said.

The Game of My Life
By Dan Gladden

I was just looking at the scoreboard, thinking about what would have to happen for me to even get up to bat. It played out in front of me as I sat there. I was the eighth batter of the inning.

What I remember about my home run and what made it so special was that I was a guy who choked up on the bat a lot of the time. Being able to read a scoreboard, though, I went up there thinking maybe I should swing for it. Power was a fastball guy. He kept the ball down. I remembered him from spring training. Our careers had sort of paralleled each other.

I looked in the Giants dugout and asked Mike Krukow and Rob Deer if I should go for the homer. They told me I shouldn't. Then Power fell behind and I knew I had to take one try at it. So I said, 'What the heck' and I dropped my hands down to the end of the handle. I wanted a fastball on the inside of the plate and high. I was looking for one pitch in one spot and I got it. I knew with the count 2-0 he was going to have to come in. He couldn't afford to walk me. I swung a 35-inch, 35-ounce bat from the knob and hit it out of there. Krukow and (Duane) Kuiper and the other guys went crazy.

It was fun for that day, though I learned that you enjoy a win one night and then get ready to play the next night. Emotionally, you've got to stay on an even keel. San Francisco was my internship, my learning ground. The players, coaches, and managers on that team helped mold me and helped me become the player that I was.

	1	2	3	4	5	6	7	8	9	R	H	E
Reds	0	1	0	3	2	0	0	0	0	6	10	0
Giants	0	0	0	1	0	0	0	0	6	7	9	1

Gladden: 5 at-bats, 2 runs, 2 hits, 1 HR, 3 RBIs

Gladden's homer helped the Giants turn around a game they should have lost but won, though 1985 was full of games they should have won but lost. Greenwald recalled another headline involving Gladden that reflected the angst San Francisco experienced that season.

"The Giants had just a terrible year, with the lowest batting average in team history," Greenwald said, "and every day Davenport said, 'I know we gonna start hittin', I know we gonna hit.' One day Gladden and Jeff Leonard get in a fight on the field during batting practice. The headline in the paper the next day says, 'Giants start hitting . . . each other.'"

In a comically appropriate twist, Candlestick Park hosted another dismal failure in 1985 with the world's first promotional launch of New Coke. The short-lived, sweeter cola formula was an instant dud in the soft drink market, but at least it ensured that the Giants weren't the stadium's only loser.

While San Francisco finished in the cellar, 33 games out of first, and the club's 100 losses set a miserable franchise record, the season imparted experience that Gladden found beneficial later in his career.

"If you look at the players on the team we had there, they'd all been winners before," Gladden said. "But they were players playing for individual satisfaction. That's the biggest difference between teams that win and the teams that don't. It showed me you don't need the big-name players. Teamwork and preparation help you win more ballgames."

Gladden soon put that lesson to work in another uniform. Just before the 1987 season started, the Giants traded him to the Minnesota Twins for three minor leaguers.

"I was a little surprised, but you knew it could happen with the number of outfielders we had in camp," Gladden said. "It turned out to be a great trade for me."

Indeed, while a resurgent San Francisco team won the National League West in 1987, Gladden and the Twins won the World Series twice in the next five years. In Game 7 of the 1991 Fall Classic against Atlanta, Gladden doubled in the bottom of the tenth and scored the series-clinching run.

Gladden's major league career ended after 1993, though he won another championship with the Tokyo Giants in 1994. During that season, the fiery competitor attracted attention by starting the first brawl of Japanese baseball in 14 years.

Not surprisingly, Gladden became a very popular figure in Minnesota, where he and his wife raised their two daughters in the city of Eden Prairie. Gladden once instructed Giants minor leaguers and later became a Twins radio broadcaster.

"I made a home here in Minnesota. This is a great place for raising your kids," he said. "I like working with my partners, John Gordon, and Jack Morris. Trying to paint a picture for the listeners as to what's going on in the ballgame is fun."

9

BOB BRENLY

"FROM THE OUTHOUSE TO THE PENTHOUSE"

POSITION: catcher

SEASONS WITH GIANTS: 1981–1989

ACCOMPLISHMENTS: All-Star in 1984; led the Giants in doubles (28) in 1984; led the Giants in home runs (19) in 1985

GAME OF HIS LIFE: September 14, 1986 versus Atlanta Braves

MANAGER ROGER CRAIG CALLED it "the greatest Humm-Baby performance of all time." Bob Brenly declared himself "the Comeback Player of the Year in one afternoon." And in the clubhouse after the game, pitcher Mike Krukow exclaimed, "This isn't your typical storybook finish, it's a novel!"

Unlike many great Giants memories, this game involved neither a pennant race nor a record-breaking achievement. Rather, the late-season contest pitted two teams far out of the race, playing for nothing but pride, and the popular Giant who starred in it suffered a cruel humiliation before rebounding to an unbelievable finale.

None of it would have happened, either, if the 32-year-old Brenly had started the game behind the plate at Candlestick as planned. But a dubious injury to a teammate forced the longtime catcher to change positions against the Braves on September 14, 1986.

"I shouldn't have even been playing third base," Brenly said. "I was supposed to catch. I had my gear on in the dugout. But Chris Brown scratched himself from the lineup about ten minutes before the game started."

Brown's long record of injuries, some of them unconvincing to his fellow Giants, led to his teammates nicknaming him "Tin Man" after the Wizard of Oz character without a heart.

"Roger Craig came up to me and said, 'You're gonna play third base,'" Brenly said. "So I took my gear off, went to my duffel bag, got my third baseman's glove, and went out there naked, as we say. I took no ground balls before the game or anything like that."

Starting pitchers Mike LaCoss and Atlanta's Charlie Puleo dueled for three uneventful frames, and there was no score when the Braves came to bat in the fourth. It proved to be the longest inning of Brenly's life. First Atlanta's Bob Horner hit a ground ball to third that Brenly botched, error number one. Left fielder Ken Griffey Sr. followed with a single, and shortstop Rafael Ramirez bunted the runners to second and third. After LaCoss walked catcher Ozzie Virgil, the bases were loaded.

If Brenly felt "naked" at third when the game began, it was nothing compared to what was coming next. Atlanta second baseman Glenn Hubbard rolled another easy grounder to third, and Brenly had a chance to start an inning-ending double play. Instead, he not only dropped the ball, enabling Hubbard to reach first, but threw wildly to the plate, letting both Horner and Griffey score. On a single play, the bungled catch and throw were errors numbers two and three, and the Braves took a 2-0 lead.

"Please, don't hit it to me anymore," Brenly silently pleaded. But it only got worse. When Puleo came to bat, the pitcher shot a bullet off the top of Brenly's glove into left field. Two more runs scored, though at least the scorekeeper ruled the play a hit. Brenly avoided another error, but not for long. That's because he booted the next ball that center fielder Dale Murphy grounded straight to him for error number four. The veteran and All-Star became the first player to commit four errors in one inning since 1942, woefully tying the major league record.

"I can't explain why it happened," Brenly said. "On Horner's ball, I looked up too soon. Then I messed up on Hubbard's grounder, but I thought

Bob Brenly's amazing comeback in a 1986 game against the Atlanta Braves won him the lasting affection of Giants fans. *AP Images*

I had a shot at the plate. I just didn't get a good grip on the ball. By the time Murphy hit the ball to me, I didn't know what had happened."

After a fly ball to center mercifully ended the inning, Brenly's teammates gave him plenty of room in the dugout. Numb, shellshocked, and more embarrassed than he'd ever been in his life, the Giant collapsed on the bench.

"Everybody that knows me knows, and my teammates all knew, that I could snap with the best of them," Brenly said. "I could break things and I could throw helmets. Everybody ran to the other end of the dugout when I came off the field, but I had this unbelievable feeling of calm, like I was in some kind of a bubble. I kept my temper."

Instead of a tantrum, Brenly had a "Humm-Baby" moment. The expression coined by Giants manager Roger Craig has various connotations, chief among them "always play hard" and "never say die."

"Roger came in and tried to change the attitude of the organization with the Humm-Baby attitude," Brenly said. "I felt I was in that mold of players. I liked to play hard, I liked to win, and I hated to lose."

Redemption began in the fifth when Brenly hit a home run to put San Francisco on the scoreboard. Teammate Bob Melvin followed with another blast, and the Giants cut their deficit to 4-2. The Braves scored again in the top of the seventh on Ramirez's two-run homer, but the Giants rallied with two out in the home half. Brenly came to bat with the bases loaded and two runs already in, facing Atlanta's fireman Gene Garber. He swung at the first two pitches, missing both badly.

"I took a big swing at two bad pitches, and the guys on the bench yelled to shorten up and put the ball in play," Brenly said. "I stayed back and got a good pitch to hit."

Brenly shot the ball into left, scoring two more and enabling San Francisco to claw all the way back into a 6-6 tie. Craig kindly moved his regular catcher behind the plate for the eighth, and the Giants' Scott Garrelts came in to pitch two shutout innings. The Braves brought in southpaw Paul Assenmacher to pitch the ninth, and the sharp rookie retired the first two

Giants before Brenly came to bat. He worked the count full and waited for the slider he knew Assenmacher would throw.

"When Bobby came up in the bottom of the ninth, the bench was alive," Craig said. "We had a feeling he was going to do it."

The goat-turned-hero of the day proved his skipper right, blasting a hanging slider to left for the most satisfying home run of his career. The 8,594 fans in attendance cheered deliriously as a beaming Brenly tossed his bat high and rounded the bases.

"That's as good a demonstration as you'll ever see of a guy not quitting when everything is going wrong," said Craig. "I don't think I've ever seen an exhibition like that when a guy's had a start like that," the manager said. "He lets in four runs, but then he drives in four—and that last one he drove in was sure something special."

In a postgame gala, Krukow enjoyed the celebration. "Hollywood couldn't write a story like that," said the pitcher. "No one would believe it."

Brenly summarized his experience perfectly. "I went from the outhouse to the penthouse," he laughed.

The Game of My Life
By Bob Brenly

In that fateful fourth inning, it just seemed like every hitter hit the ball to me, even besides the errors I made. I didn't want to see another ground ball. I would have hid under the bag if I could have. I can laugh about it now, but I wasn't too pleased about the four errors at the time.

It just felt so strange. When I hit the home run to put us on the board, and got a base hit with the bases loaded a little later to drive in a couple more runs, it was like somebody else was doing it and I was up above the stadium watching myself do these things. Even in the ninth inning when I hit that home run to win the game, it felt like I had no control of it. I don't know what you would call it. Sometimes athletes get in a zone.

I'm very glad for it now. What could have been just a hideously awful day in the big leagues turned it into kind of a rallying point. If you can come back from something like that, you can come back from anything. I think in a lot of ways, that was a game that reflected Roger more than anything else, and that Humm-Baby, never-say-die attitude.

I think I obviously had much better games, but it became the game I was known for in my career with the Giants. There were maybe 10,000 people at that game, and over the years, I've talked to a lot more people than that who said they were there that day.

	1	2	3	4	5	6	7	8	9	R	H	E
Braves	0	0	0	4	0	0	2	0	0	6	8	1
Giants	0	0	0	0	2	0	4	0	1	7	11	5

Brenly: 4 errors, 5 at-bats, 2 runs, 3 hits, 2 HR, 4 RBIs

Brenly's baseball resume is uniquely accomplished and diverse. He coached the Giants under both Craig and Dusty Baker. As a rookie manager, he led the Arizona Diamondbacks to the 2001 World Series championship. He's also become a popular broadcaster on radio and television, working in San Francisco, Arizona, Chicago, and for the Fox network.

His rags-to-riches game, though, occupies a special place in his memory. As a coach and manager, Brenly has used the game as the basis for an effective pep-talk.

"When we had guys who had bad days individually, I talked to them in the middle of the game," Brenly said. "'Hey, you think you've got it bad. You made two errors in six innings, I made four errors in one inning!' When you tell them the capper, a lot of the younger players who weren't familiar with my playing career, they can't believe it until I break out the videotape."

In fact, the story has even gained attention in circles far removed from baseball. For Brenly, it's a rewarding legacy of an astounding day.

"I've gotten letters from ministers all over the country who've used the story as an inspirational sermon on Sundays," Brenly said. "That doesn't feel bad. I guess it's better than having people talk about you in a bar at two o'clock in the morning. If people use something I've done in my career as hopefully a way to inspire people to continue to push hard and grind when things are at their worst, I'm a little flattered by that."

10
DON ROBINSON

THE "CAVEMAN" WHO DEFIED EXTINCTION

POSITION: pitcher

SEASONS WITH GIANTS: 1987–1991

ACCOMPLISHMENTS: led Giants in ERA (2.45) in 1988; led National League with the fewest walks per nine innings (1.69) in 1989; won the Silver Slugger award in 1989 and 1990

GAME OF HIS LIFE: September 28, 1987 versus San Diego Padres

DON ROBINSON HAD A surgically repaired shoulder, elbow, knee, and toe. He had an arthritic hip. The man his teammates called "the Caveman" took some 200 cortisone shots during his career.

"The guy was a cartoon," teammate Mike Krukow said. "The more stitches and cuts he had, the more he liked going out there and playing. If you took all the scars on him and laid them together inch by inch, you'd get a line that stretched from San Jose to Palo Alto."

Robinson wouldn't let any ailment stop him against the Padres on September 28, 1987. The pitcher carried the Giants to their biggest win in 16 years the same way he carried himself through 15 injury-filled seasons: with his arm, his bat, and enough grit and determination to defy belief and reason.

Manager Roger Craig's "Humm-Baby" Giants had risen from cellar dwellers into contenders into division leaders. San Francisco was one win away from a National League West championship, its first since 1971, when the club visited San Diego during the season's final week.

The Giants' Kevin Mitchell and Candy Maldonado hit safely in the third to produce a run against Padres starter Eric Show. In the fourth, Jose Uribe singled ahead of a hot Jeffrey Leonard, who clubbed a pinch-hit homer to extend San Francisco's lead. But Giants pitcher Dave Dravecky struggled too, allowing two hits and a walk in the Padres' third. Randy Ready homered off the lefty in the fourth, followed by a Tony Gwynn RBI single to tie the game, 3-3.

When San Diego brought in southpaw Mark Davis to pitch in the fifth, Craig countered with the switch-hitting Chili Davis off the bench. The manager's intuition paid off, as the Giants pinch hitter smashed another home run on a 3-1 pitch to put San Francisco ahead, 4-3.

Enter Robinson, then 30, summoned from the bullpen far earlier than usual to replace a tiring Dravecky. "I usually came in the eighth, but Dravecky got himself in trouble so Roger called down and told them to get me up," the Giant said. "I didn't have my shoes tied, I didn't have socks up, I didn't even have my knee brace on. I had to do all that stuff real fast, throw six or seven pitches in the pen, and then I was in the game."

Robinson shut down the Padres quickly in the San Diego fifth, walking first baseman John Kruk but enticing catcher Benito Santiago, a future Giant, to ground into a double play. Robinson pitched through a rare Robby Thompson error in the sixth to retire the side without damage once more. But the Padres bullpen dug in, too. Mitchell and Maldonado singled in the sixth, though the Giants failed to score again against Mark Davis. A rally fizzled in the seventh when San Diego's left fielder Carmelo Martinez gunned down Thompson trying to stretch a double into a triple.

Robinson clung to a one-run lead when he started his third inning of work in the bottom of the seventh. The Padres, 21 games behind in the West, were long since out of the division race, but they refused to let the Giants clinch against them easily. Martinez singled to left and the speedy Stan Jefferson entered the game to run for him. The pinch runner immediately stole second, soon to score on a Santiago triple. Robinson marooned the catcher at third, but the damage was done. San Diego had tied the game, 4-4.

Robinson had pitched three innings, allowing two hits and a run, and was due to lead off the Giants' eighth. Most relievers would gladly head for the showers after such a worthy outing, but then most relievers are nothing like the Caveman.

"I begged Roger to let me hit," said Robinson. "Lance McCullers was in for the Padres. I told Roger that I like to hit sliders and breaking balls. I wasn't much of a fastball hitter. I had to wait for a breaking ball to hit it. Most pitchers are going to throw other pitchers breaking balls. I knew that boy would throw me a slider."

That left Craig with a tough decision to make: Send a tired and battered reliever out to hit in a high-stakes tied game, or pinch hit? Managers have lost jobs for less, but Craig trusted his intuition and his pitcher once more. Robinson worked the count full, 3-2. Then McCullers threw the slider, a hanger, and Robinson whacked it just over the left-field fence for his first homer in two years.

"I knew it had a chance unless somebody made a spectacular play," said Robinson. "I'm not exactly a home run hitter, but I got that one good."

The Giants took a 5-4 lead, and needed six more outs to end their playoff drought. Craig had fresh arms in the bullpen but the skipper stuck with Robinson. "Robinson was a bulldog out there," Craig explained. "He's done it for us ever since he came over. He's the guy I wanted to have in there, and I wanted to keep him there."

In the eighth, Robinson mowed down the Padres, 1-2-3, on a grounder, a strikeout, and a pop-up. The Giants went down quickly in their half of the ninth, and the pitcher was right back on the hill.

"I wasn't tired," Robinson said. "I was too pumped up to be tired."

Gwynn, who made a Hall of Fame career out of ground-ball singles to left, cracked another one to lead off the ninth. Robinson got the first out

Don Robinson pitched five innings in relief and hit a home run as the Giants clinched the division in 1987. *Stephen Dunn/Getty Images*

when Shane Mack bunted Gwynn to second. Jefferson grounded out, but moved the tying run to third.

With two outs and the left-handed slugger Kruk coming to bat, Craig walked to the mound to speak with his pitcher. Would the manager pull Robinson for the southpaw Craig Lefferts, warmed and ready in the pen? Craig had a different message for Robinson. "The champagne's on ice, big boy," the skipper told him. The pitcher was glad to hear it, because he had a plan in mind if the manager had tried to take the ball. "I wouldn't have given it to him," Robinson joked. "I would have tackled him first."

Kruk drove a ball deep to left, and San Francisco got a scare as Leonard ran back to the wall. Then the left fielder came in a few steps and put it away. The game was over, the Giants were NL West champions, and a frenzied pack of players swarmed Robinson on the mound.

The Game of My Life
By Don Robinson

I came to the Giants at the July 31 trading deadline that year. I cried when I was traded. I'd won a championship with the Pirates and I was very comfortable there. The Giants' doggone ballpark was so cold all the time, and plus being from West Virginia, my parents could come up and see me in Pittsburgh anytime. In San Francisco, 3,000 miles across the country, they never got to see me. But after a month or two I kind of fit right in. It was good to be in contention, and it's always fun to play in September when it means something.

I never had much trouble with the Padres. My first big league shutout was against the Padres in 1978. They were one of the teams I felt confident about when I pitched against them. But I got lucky with the double play in the fifth. Santiago was an aggressive hitter who would swing at a pitch in the dirt.

When I was due to bat in the eighth, it put Roger in a bad spot. If I struck out, I'm sure the press would've really got on him, especially if I gave a run up in the ninth inning and we'd lost the game. But it worked out for both of us. He hung me a slider and I hit it into the left-field bleachers. And Roger didn't get buried for letting me hit.

In the ninth inning, I hung a 1-2 splitter to Kruk. When he hit that ball, I thought the game was at least tied. I thought it might even be a home run. Kruk had had some success against me and he'd hit a few home runs off me in the past. Leonard ran to the wall and looked up and deked me. But then he came back and caught the ball, and that was it.

	1	2	3	4	5	6	7	8	9	R	H	E
Giants	0	0	1	2	1	0	0	1	0	5	12	2
Padres	0	0	1	2	0	0	1	0	0	4	10	1

Robinson: win, 5 innings pitched, 3 hits, 1 run, 2 walks, 2 strikeouts

---

Among the 29,844 in attendance at Jack Murphy Stadium were a significant number of delighted Giants fans. Some of them joyfully ran across the field, leading to a confrontation with park security and arrests. In the Bay Area, thousands of fans in sports bars and family rooms cheered in long-awaited exultation. Meanwhile, the rapturous Giants soaked the visitors clubhouse with champagne and beer. The club had come a long way from its 100-loss nadir in 1985, and only a handful of its current players had ever reached the playoffs before.

"I remember when we couldn't win ballgames when we needed to," said Chili Davis. "Now, even the pitcher goes out there and hits a home run. It just goes to show you what changes have been made in the organization."

Robinson's teammates nicknamed him "the Caveman" because of his muscle-bound frame, hairy features, and scarred body. He came to like the moniker "because it shows I'm a gamer, that I've overcome a lot of injuries," he said.

In fact, Robinson once assumed his Caveman persona for a magazine cover shot, donning a fur and a necklace of saber-toothed tiger teeth, and holding an armful of stone baseballs in one hand and an enormous club-like "bat" in the other. "I felt kind of stupid in that outfit, but I'm the Caveman, so I had to do it," the Giant said.

Robinson played for the Giants as both a starter and reliever through 1991, continuing to tough out enough injuries to sideline an entire pitching staff. Among other challenges, he had reconstructive surgery on a badly stretched medial collateral ligament in 1989.

"All that's left of Robinson is the biggest competitive heart I've seen in my lifetime," said Dr. Jack Failla, his frequently employed surgeon. "I'm not trying to canonize the guy, but he has more guts than common sense. If he had only one and a half legs, he'd go out there and pitch."

Robinson was once asked why he continued his losing battle against pain for so long. "I just love the competition," he replied.

"If there was ever a body built to absorb medical abuse, it was his," Krukow said. "He never bitched about being hurt. He didn't care. He could break his humerus in a compound fracture and still give you three solid innings."

Robinson left the game after short stints with the Angels and Phillies in 1992. In his career, the gutsy and versatile pitcher won 109 games and saved 57 more. Retired in Bradenton, Florida, Robinson still has on his wall a picture of the Giants' celebration on September 28, 1987.

"I couldn't jump very high but I jumped up," he recalled. "We had a big party after the game at the hotel. It was good. I'd been through it in '79 (with Pittsburgh), but we had a bunch of players in San Francisco who had never won a division or reached the World Series before. Players take it for granted that they are going to get there but most of them never do."

11
MIKE KRUKOW

"LIKE NO OTHER GAME"

POSITION: pitcher

SEASONS WITH GIANTS: 1983–1989

ACCOMPLISHMENTS: All-Star in 1986; led Giants in wins in 1984 (11) and 1986 (20); led Giants in ERA in 1985 (3.38) and 1986 (3.05); led Giants in strikeouts in 1983 (136), 1984 (141), 1985 (150), and 1986 (178)

GAME OF HIS LIFE: October 10, 1987 versus St. Louis Cardinals

---

CHILI DAVIS GOT IT started when he called St. Louis a "cow town." Hundreds of defiant Cardinals fans proudly rang cowbells for the rest of the series. Then pitcher Dave Dravecky threw the finest game of his career, a two-hit shutout on enemy territory. And San Francisco's Jeffrey Leonard tore apart the St. Louis pitching staff, hitting home runs in each of the first three contests. His slow trots around the bases so infuriated the Cardinals that pitcher Bob Forsch beamed him in the third game.

"There was no doubt that Forsch hit him intentionally," said Bob Brenly, then a Giants catcher. "Looking back, if we had it to do over again, we should have run out there and kicked their asses."

So exciting and dramatic was the 1987 National League Championship Series that years later, San Francisco's players are still fired up about it. One is a Giant who never left the franchise: Mike Krukow, San Francisco's starting pitcher in an "awesome" Game 4.

"The best time for a major league player going into the playoffs is the first time. For most of us, it was our first time in 1987," Krukow said. "It was like no other game I ever pitched in."

San Francisco needed Krukow's best in the worst way, because the Giants already trailed St. Louis by a game in the series. After the teams split the first two contests at Busch Stadium, the Cardinals came from behind to win Game 3 at Candlestick Park.

"The first three were all well-played, emotional games," Krukow said. "Going into the fourth game, (manager) Roger Craig was in a quandary about what to do because he didn't know how long I could go."

San Francisco's ace a year before, "Kruk" struggled with a torn labrum all through 1987. For a time, the 35-year-old questioned whether he would make the postseason roster at all, and if he did, how much he could contribute.

"Go as far as you can and don't save anything," his skipper told him. "I've got guys in the pen to back you up. We can't go down three games to one at home."

While the October 10 contest became Krukow's undisputed career highlight, the tall right-hander had to scratch and claw to stay in it. His gritty performance and the Giants' clutch hitting and defense all contributed in a back-and-forth dogfight of a game. Krukow pitched through an error and a walk in the first, inducing Willie McGee to fly out to center to escape without damage. In the second, St. Louis came right back at the pitcher, cracking four straight singles to take a 2-0 lead. The only pitch Kruk regretted was a fat 0-2 offering to the pitcher, Danny Cox, who knocked the ball to left to drive in the first run.

With one out, the Cardinals still had two men on base when Ozzie Smith stepped in to face Krukow for the second time. Smith shot a low line drive straight to the second baseman. Robby Thompson caught it at his shoes and immediately fired to first, beating Vince Coleman back to the bag. The double play ended the St. Louis second and gave new life to the Giants starting pitcher.

Mike Krukow went the distance in his first and only career postseason appearance against the St. Louis Cardinals. *SF Giants*

"It was red alert in the bullpen," Krukow said. "There were sparks coming from out there. But Thompson's great play gave me a chance to regroup."

Krukow bore down in the Cardinals' third and fourth, retiring six straight batters in two perfect frames. San Francisco's offense struck in the bottom of the fourth, when Thompson hit a two-out homer to put the home team on the scoreboard. But a relentless St. Louis lineup tested the Giants again in the fifth. After Coleman singled for the second straight time, Smith came to bat with a chance to avenge his earlier double play. A future Hall of Famer, Smith laced a line drive into right that appeared to all concerned to be a sure base hit. Charging in hard to get it was San Francisco's Mike Aldrete. The diving right fielder snared the ball just above the grass to ice a potential Cardinals rally.

"Every time they'd get going with a dead bird or a line drive, we'd make the defensive play," Krukow said. "When Aldrete came in on the sinking line drive and took away the hit, to me, that was the turning point in the game."

San Francisco proved him right in their half of the fifth, starting with Kevin Mitchell's two-out double to bring up the slugger Leonard. The Cardinals didn't walk "Hac-Man" this time, though they would quickly wish they had. After his homers in the previous games, Leonard ran the bases in slow motion holding one arm motionless at his side. St. Louis players and fans perceived his "one-flap down" home run trots as taunts, leading to loud booing and anti-Leonard rhetoric at Busch Stadium.

"He tucked an elbow in and ran around the bags. He was just brash and arrogant," said Krukow, Leonard's longtime teammate. "It's one thing to do something like that, but you'd better back it up, and he did. He put up just an unbelievable series."

This time, Leonard hit Cox's first-pitch heater a mile high into the Candlestick night. The left fielder Coleman drifted back to the warning track, and then to the wall. He leaped as the high arcing ball just cleared his glove and the fence. The wind-aided shot gave San Francisco a 3-2 lead.

"He popped it up," Krukow said. "That was a divine intervention home run."

Angry at the wind, the ballpark, and Leonard, the Cardinals agreed with that assessment. "He didn't hit the ball real well. He didn't hit it well at all," griped catcher Tony Pena. St. Louis manager Whitey Herzog, fuming about the play after the game, called the big fly "a can of mush."

After Kruk got to pitch with the lead for the first time, ground balls became the hurler's best friend for the rest of the evening. "Every inning was a puzzle," the pitcher recalled. "My stuff early was different than my stuff later. I just went with what was working."

After Pena singled to lead off the seventh, the curveball-throwing Krukow got Coleman to ground a comebacker straight to him. The Giant started another double play, this time from pitcher to shortstop to first.

Perhaps the Cardinals' highlight arrived in the bottom of the frame, when Hac-Man walked ahead of first baseman Will Clark. When "the Thrill" ripped a double into left, his teammate tried to score. Pena got the ball in time and tagged Leonard on the neck as forcefully as he could.

"He hit me, but he didn't hurt me," Leonard scoffed.

"If he comes to the plate again, I'll hit him even harder," Pena vowed.

More Krukow magic followed in the eighth when second baseman Tom Herr connected for a one-out single. This time, the pitcher induced first baseman Dan Driessen to ground to Clark, who started another twin killing, the third of the night.

Fighting all night without his best stuff, Krukow started the ninth, leading 4-2 after Brenly's eighth-inning homer provided an insurance run. McGee led off with ground ball to first. Clark chased it down and threw to Krukow as he hustled to the bag. Third baseman Terry Pendleton singled to center for the Cardinals' 11th base runner. Yet again, St. Louis brought the tying run to the plate in right fielder Curt Ford. But like they had all night, Krukow and his defense stymied the Cardinals threat. Ford grounded the ball to Thompson, who started San Francisco's fourth double play.

The ballgame was over, and the National League Championship Series was tied. Krukow had pitched a complete-game win in his first and only playoff appearance. A record 57,997 fans thunderously applauded the Giants' first postseason win at Candlestick since 1971.

The Game of My Life
By Mike Krukow

I had won 20 in '86 and I was the Opening Day starter in '87, but that season was a series of nightmares for me dealing with arm injuries. I was starting to get my timing back. I didn't have great stuff, but what I had, I could command. I took a good set of mechanics into the game. I knew I was going to do well.

There were 57,000 people there who were all totally into it. Every ball they agonized over, every strike they applauded. They were into it. It was a great vibe, man.

We fell behind in the second inning. I gave up an 0-2 hit to Cox and they took a 2-0 lead. So I came back in the dugout after the inning and said to myself, "That's all they're gonna get. If we score more than two runs, we're gonna win."

From a pitcher's perspective, it was one of those games where I knew 3-4 pitches into each at-bat how it was going to go. There were those great defensive plays by Aldrete and Thompson, energizing me, the team, the crowd, and it all just snowballed.

We had guys in the pen if I had faltered. They were warming up from the second inning on. They probably threw as many pitches in the pen as I did in the game. But Roger could see that I wasn't coming out. He just knew that I had locked in.

After the 27th out, 57,000 people just went off. It was the most incredible experience of my professional career. That night meant so much to our organization, our team, and our town. I still hear from people today who were at that game, telling me how special it was and sharing it with me.

As an athlete, you want to be remembered. When they start smiling and you start smiling listening to them, and you've both still got that vibe from 20 years ago, that's pretty sweet. That's the game that endeared me to the Bay Area. I think that's the one game I will always be remembered for as a Giant.

	1	2	3	4	5	6	7	8	9	R	H	E
Cardinals	0	2	0	0	0	0	0	0	0	2	9	0
Giants	0	0	0	1	2	0	1	0	x	4	9	2

Krukow: win, 9 innings pitched, 9 hits, 2 runs, 1 walk, 3 strikeouts

---

San Francisco won Game 5 to take a 3-2 series lead, needing just one more game to advance to the World Series. But the orange and black failed to score in the last two contests in St. Louis, losing the National League pennant to the din of countless clanging cowbells.

"It was such a tough loss. Game 7 was excruciating to us," Krukow said. "We were miserable because we lost there and couldn't leave St. Louis that night. At the hotel we had to listen to those goddamn horns honking all night long."

Still, 1987 was a remarkable year for the division champion Giants. "We've got nothing to be ashamed of," manager Roger Craig told his team. "Not many people thought we would get this far."

Krukow never expected to get so far with the Giants when the Phillies traded him to San Francisco in December 1982. Initially, the pitcher was dismayed to move to an unsuccessful franchise from Philadelphia's World Series-bound team.

"I was disappointed," the longtime Giant admitted. "I was really happy with Philadelphia and the people I was playing with, like Mike Schmidt,

Pete Rose, Steve Carlton, Gary Matthews, and Garry Maddox. When you're in a situation like that, you don't want to take a step back. I didn't think we had a team that would match up with the Phils in '83."

Indeed, San Francisco struggled greatly for the next three years, but Krukow stayed long enough to see the organization turn around.

"When (general manager) Al Rosen and Roger Craig took over, things began to change," he said. "I developed an appreciation for the fans, and how really desperate this Bay Area was to resurrect the image of this team. I found out I was in the middle of this effort and I could have a lot do with it."

During his seven years in a San Francisco uniform, Krukow led the team in wins and ERA twice and in strikeouts four times.

"Mike threw a very good curveball, sinker, and slider and he could pop his fastball. He mixed it up and had good command of all four pitches, and good movement," recalled teammate Atlee Hammaker. "The thing that stood out to me was that he was such a great competitor. He never let up, no matter what kind of stuff he had."

After retiring as a player following San Francisco's pennant-winning 1989 season, Krukow began a long and successful run as a Giants broadcaster. An Emmy award winner, Krukow provides color commentary on radio and television, often paired with play-by-play man Duane Kuiper, his old teammate and best friend.

Between their broadcasts, commercials, video game voiceovers, and talking bobbleheads, the popular "Kruk and Kuip" have become a Bay Area institution.

"As upset as I was in 1983, it turned out to be the greatest thing that ever happened to me," Krukow said. "It's been unbelievable what has happened. I feel lucky to go to work every day."

12

DAVE DRAVECKY

"A MIRACLE"

POSITION: pitcher

SEASONS WITH GIANTS: 1987–1989

ACCOMPLISHMENTS: pitched complete game shutout in 1987 National League Championship Series; started Opening Day in 1988; won Willie Mac Award in 1989

GAME OF HIS LIFE: August 10, 1989 versus Cincinnati Reds

BASEBALL'S GREATEST MEMORIES INCLUDE more than just balls and strikes. On rare occasions, the diamond provides a stage for astonishing moments that transcend the game.

Dave Dravecky's miraculous comeback from cancer in 1989 belongs at the top of this list. The pitcher's fight to pitch and win in the big leagues again awed all who witnessed it and redefined the possible for countless others who have struggled with cancer and other ailments.

"The power of the story has to do with the fact that it's about more than Dave Dravecky the baseball player," Dravecky said. "It's about a journey through pain and suffering that touches so many of us where we live. As a result, we want to hear stories that will encourage, inspire and help us."

Acquired from the Padres in a 1987 trade, Dravecky helped the Giants capture their first division championship in 16 years and pitched a shutout in the playoffs against the St. Louis Cardinals.

But in 1988, Dravecky investigated a lump he had noticed in his pitching arm. Dave and his wife Janice Dravecky prayed as they waited for a prognosis. Doctors discovered a cancerous tumor. Dravecky needed surgery, they said. With luck, he might be able to play catch with his son again one day. "Outside a miracle, you'll never pitch again," one doctor told him.

"I went through a progression almost every individual takes after getting diagnosed with cancer," Dravecky said. "First it was denial. Then I became fearful because I didn't want to die. Will I survive this, or will this take my life? I started experiencing all kinds of emotions."

A ten-hour surgery removed the tumor and half his deltoid muscle in October. Doctors also froze his humerus bone through a procedure called cryosurgery in hopes of killing cancer cells.

"That was pretty intense," Dravecky said. "My recovery initially was really slow. I began therapy with no mobility whatsoever. I could not even move my arm. I started from scratch with a therapist moving it through a range of motion for me."

Dravecky visited the Giants clubhouse during spring training in 1989 with an impressive scar to show his teammates. "Man, you look like Jaws took a bite out of you," left fielder Kevin Mitchell said. But by then he was able to play catch.

As his mobility and strength increased, Dravecky amazed his doctors and gradually improved to the point that they approved a rehabilitation plan to attempt what had once seemed impossible: a return to baseball.

"Dave, you shouldn't be able to do what you're doing. I don't understand how it's happening," said Dr. Gordon Campbell. "So you might as well take your chances. Go ahead and throw."

Dravecky, 33, began a grueling workout regimen that pushed him to his limit and beyond.

"It was long, frustrating, exciting, and exhilarating. There were times when I hit the wall and moments of wanting to quit and moments of extreme highs. All of those things and more were part of this process," he said.

Dave Dravecky defied the odds with his comeback from cancer and win against the Reds. *SF Giants*

"Lots of people have asked why I didn't just put baseball behind me and focus on getting healthy," he said. "That would have meant living the rest of my life wondering if I could have done it. I couldn't do that."

By June of 1989, Dravecky was throwing batting practice for the Giants. He began a minor league stint in July, winning all three games he pitched. Each of them drew crowds far greater than usual in Stockton and Reno. The unprecedented story of a big league pitcher coming back from cancer was catching on, but no one could imagine what was still to come.

"Pack your bags," a team official told him after his third start. "You're going to the major leagues." Dravecky took all his minor league teammates, their wives and their girlfriends out to dinner to celebrate.

Manager Roger Craig chose Dravecky to start on August 10 against Cincinnati. The assignment was not charity; the Giants fought for a pennant in 1989. Nor could Dravecky expect sympathy from the Reds. "He's back, and it's great for him," said manager Pete Rose. "I hope he loses."

As Dravecky prepared for an outing momentous for him and his team, an even greater aspect of the event came into focus. A fundraising drive had begun to support the care of Alex Vlahos, a six-year-old boy fighting leukemia and in need of bone marrow transplants which require expensive donor screening. Donors pledged more than $1,000 for every pitch Dravecky threw in his comeback game. So even before the southpaw took the mound, his story had started helping others.

A robust crowd of 34,810 filled Candlestick Park on a Thursday afternoon to see one of the most inspirational events in the history of sports.

The Game of My Life
By Dave Dravecky

I really tried to keep things as calm as possible and went to the park with that in mind. Everybody in the clubhouse played right into that, messing around, ribbing me and trying to keep the environment normal. When I walked onto the field and started warming up, everybody started yelling like crazy and all the media took pictures. I looked at my catcher Terry Kennedy and pounded my hand on my heart to show how my pulse was hammering. "Me too," he said.

The umpire said "Play ball," and all of a sudden the crowd erupts and I get standing ovation. There was another ovation every inning that day. Obviously this was not the norm. It felt like a World Series game. It was incredible and such a special day.

Standing on the mound, I was overwhelmed with thankfulness. I didn't know what God's big plan was in the midst of my story unfolding with cancer, but I was really thankful for people He placed in my life and who played such a big part in my well being.

The rhythm I had throughout the game was no different than I had before in the end of '87 or Opening Day of '88. I had good control. My guys gave me the support I needed. Matt Williams crushed a fastball into the left field seats. I remember striking out Ron Oester and I remember Pete Rose got thrown out for arguing balls and strikes.

I was so mad that Luis Quinones hit a home run off me! Terry came up to me and said, "Stinking Quinones messed up our script!" But we laughed because we still won the game.

The greatest part of all to think back on is the support of my teammates and the organization. That's been really special to me over the years. I still look in the mirror and see myself as a San Francisco Giant.

That game meant so much more than just the game because it was also about a young boy fighting for his life and a community that rallied around a family in great need, like my teammates rallied around me. There's a wonderful lesson there: we can't do this thing called life alone.

	1	2	3	4	5	6	7	8	9	R	H	E
Reds	0	0	0	0	0	0	0	3	0	3	4	0
Giants	0	1	1	0	2	0	0	0	x	4	5	0

Dravecky: win, 8 innings pitched, 4 hits, 3 runs, 1 walk, 5 strikeouts

Giants fans showered Dravecky with a dozen standing ovations. Janice Dravecky cried through the entire game. Even hardened sportswriters were moved to tears. Nearly $200,000 was raised for Alex Vlahos.

"When I first saw his arm, I didn't think he'd ever pick up a baseball again. I've seen a lot of things in baseball, but I can't remember a game with more drama than this one," Craig said after the game. "I saw, with my own eyes, a miracle."

Even so, it did not end the adversity. The Giant returned to the mound five days later to pitch in Montreal. His humerus, perhaps weakened by the cryosurgery, snapped in mid-pitch. The terrible setback was the first of many including the return of cancer. Within two years, doctors were forced to amputate Dravecky's left arm and shoulder. By that time, young Alex had died.

Dravecky struggled with depression after these events but took comfort in the words of a teammate. "What God is doing is giving you a platform to share His love with those who hurt," pitcher Bob Knepper had told him.

"I realized something was going on in my life a whole lot bigger than baseball," Dravecky said.

So in 1991, Dave and Janice founded a non-profit ministry now called Endurance that provides spiritual and emotional assistance to those suffering from illness or loss. On an office wall, a picture of Dravecky holding Alex Vlahos shows how it all began. Based in Lone Tree, Colorado, the support group has responded to thousands of requests.

Dravecky has also expressed his message of hope to uncounted thousands more through his books and frequent motivational speaking engagements. More than two decades later, people are still eager to hear the tale, which both amazes and gratifies him.

"I can't tell you how many people have said to me, 'Your story inspired me in my own struggle,'" Dravecky said. "Looking back, it really was all worth it."

13

WILL CLARK

"WE NEEDED TO WIN"

POSITION: first base

SEASONS WITH GIANTS: 1986–1993

ACCOMPLISHMENTS: six-time All-Star; led National League in games (162), RBIs (109), and walks (100) in 1988; led National League in runs (104) in 1989; led National League in slugging percentage (.536) in 1991; won Silver Slugger award in 1989 and 1991; won Gold Glove in 1991

GAME OF HIS LIFE: October 9, 1989 versus Chicago Cubs

THEY DIDN'T CALL HIM "the Thrill" for nothing. When Will Clark played first base for the Giants, he electrified San Francisco with his swing and his sneer.

First, the swing. Starting in his first major league at-bat when he homered off Nolan Ryan's 100-mph fastball, Clark powered the Giants for years with his bat and a seemingly endless string of game-winning hits. And the sneer? Clark was Clint Eastwood in cleats, only louder and more high strung. The first baseman played the game with a cocky swagger. He was known to shout profanities in front of spectators and television cameras even when the Giants won, and when they lost, look out. "You will never, ever, do that to me again!" he screamed at a pitcher who got him out in a clutch situation.

"The big thing people say to me is, 'Why don't you ever smile?'" the Giant once said. "Well, I'm too interested in trying to beat somebody right now to smile."

During his first four seasons, Clark became a two-time All-Star and a National League leader in games, walks, runs, and RBIs. He came within a hair of winning an MVP trophy and a batting title. After the Giants lost a franchise-worst 100 games in 1985, Clark brought the success-starved club back with a vengeance, leading San Francisco to two National League West championships.

Then on October 9, 1989, the Thrill pushed the team to a height it hadn't reached in 27 years. San Francisco played the Chicago Cubs in the National League Championship Series for the pennant and a trip to the World Series, leading by three games to one.

In the first NLCS contest at Wrigley Field, Clark had exploded with a single, a double, a solo homer, and a grand slam, scoring four runs and driving in six. The Giants took the opener, 11-3, and pushed their lead by winning two of the next three contests. All the while, their star first baseman kept knocking the cover off the ball, hitting an unbelievable .625 through the first four games.

"You get into a situation where the ball looks real big," said Clark, then 25 years old. "I've got a lot of confidence—I feel like I'm going to get a hit every time. My concentration level is extremely high."

San Francisco had one chance to win the pennant at home before the series moved back to Wrigley for the potential sixth and seventh contests. Following the team's miserable playoff collapse in St. Louis two years earlier, this time the Giants were highly motivated to clinch the title at Candlestick.

"We wanted to wrap it up right then and take care of business at home," Clark recalled. "No way we wanted to go back to Chicago."

After four high-scoring games in which the teams combined for 47 runs, Game 5 was a hard-fought pitchers' duel. Rick "Big Daddy" Reuschel, a master of off-speed pitches and a 17-game winner in 1989, pitched his way out of several jams, scattering seven hits in eight innings. The Giants defense supported him with two double plays, and the pitcher held the Cubs to a single unearned run.

Will Clark hit a staggering .650 in the 1989 playoffs and shattered five series records. *Brace Photo*

Chicago's Mike Bielecki appeared sharper, opening the game with three perfect frames. Clark's single in the fourth was the first San Francisco hit, though he didn't score, and the Giants trailed through six innings, 1-0. But Clark struck again to lead off the seventh, driving a ball down the right-field line. Chicago right fielder Andre Dawson could only tip it with his glove, and the ball bounced into the corner, permitting Clark to dash to third.

"The ball just kept sailing away from him," Clark said. "I was around first, and he hadn't even gotten to the ball yet to throw it to the cutoff man, so I just kept running."

Moments later, Kevin Mitchell hit a fly ball to center for a sacrifice fly, easily deep enough to score Clark and tie the game. As their hero raced home with the tying run, 62,084 nervous fans inside the park came unglued. Many of them weren't yet born when San Francisco had last won a pennant. The pitcher recovered, but the damage was done, and the Giants came back for more in the eighth.

Bielecki retired pinch hitter Ken Oberkfell and struck out shortstop Jose Uribe to open the frame. Then San Francisco's Candy Maldonado dueled for ten pitches, finally drawing a two-out walk. Center fielder Brett Butler worked the count full in his at-bat as well before coaxing another base on balls.

Chicago's bullpen went to red alert as the starting pitcher seemed to run out of gas. Cubs manager Don Zimmer permitted Bielecki to face Robby Thompson but the decision was a mistake; the hurler walked the Giants second baseman on four pitches.

"I guess I was a little tired. I wanted to get that last out and take it from there. I tried to reach back, but there was nothing there," Bielecki said. "I missed with the first two pitches, then I just lost it."

That brought up the searing-hot Clark with the bases loaded in a tied game. Facing a doomsday scenario with the World Series on the line, Zimmer went to his best fireman. Mitch Williams saved 36 games for Chicago in 1989, but he was so unpredictable that his teammates called him "Wild Thing." Opponents worried about his erratic control and feared to dig in against him. A joke about Williams circulated the league: "You can't hit him, but he might hit you."

Ballparks don't usually play theme music for visiting players, but while the pitcher warmed up, the Candlestick sound system blasted his trademark tune at ear-splitting volume: "Wild thing, you make my heart sing, you make everything, groovy." Meanwhile, Clark and Mitchell conferenced by the on-deck circle.

"Remember this guy?" Mitchell asked.

"Sure do," Clark said.

"Go get it done," Mitchell said.

"It's done," Clark replied.

"Then he got that sneer on his face, that Clint Eastwood look of his," Mitchell remembered. "Once he said it was done, I knew it was done."

A flamethrower pure and simple, Williams started Clark with a fastball on the outside corner, called strike one. Clark fouled off the next heater, and down 0-2, dug in for the battle that immortalized him in Giants lore.

"There were 62,000 fans yelling and screaming, and the only thing I was worried about was the baseball," Clark said. "I couldn't even tell you what Williams' eyes looked like, or if he had a beard. I'm just thinking about that ball, that's all."

Williams, who did have a beard, fired heater after heater, and Clark fought off each one. The at-bat reached its sixth pitch.

"The more he fouled off those pitches, the more I thought Will had him," said Giants manager Roger Craig. "It was one of those moments of destiny."

Then Wild Thing threw a 99-mph fastball across the letters, and the Thrill hammered it up the middle and into center field. Maldonado and Butler sprinted home as pandemonium broke out at Candlestick and across the Bay Area. In the hours that followed, teammates and opponents would canonize Clark's ability in the highest possible terms, but all that had to wait. The Giants led, 3-1, but still needed three outs for their first National League championship since 1962. The Cubs didn't go quietly. In the ninth, Giants pitcher Steve Bedrosian quickly retired Chicago's Luis Salazar and Shawon Dunston, and for a moment it appeared the closer would nail it down easily. Then the Cubs roared back with three straight singles from Curt Wilkerson, Mitch Webster, and Jerome Walton.

"My fastball didn't have a lot of giddy-up on it," Bedrosian admitted. "A lot of those pitches came from the heart, not from the arm."

Chicago scored a run and put the tying run on second base. Giants fans were still loud, but anxious. Then a weary Bedrosian got an encouraging message from—who else?—his star teammate at first base.

"It's your game!" Clark screamed at his pitcher. "And you're going to win it!"

Clark's words gave the closer a lift. "I liked that," Bedrosian later said. "I felt like, 'Come on, Will, yell at me some more.'"

Next up was the Cubs' great second baseman, Ryne Sandberg, a perennial All-Star. Losing speed on his fastball, Bedrosian threw him a change-up, and the future Hall of Famer rolled a ground ball to second. The sure-handed Thompson scooped it up and threw to Clark, and the ballgame was over. Candlestick erupted like a beer bottle that had been shaken for 27 years and finally popped open. During their 32 years in San Francisco, the Giants had never clinched a league championship or even a division title at home, and fans rocked the park to the rafters. Delirious players in orange and black tore about like madmen. All of them had a hand in bringing about the victory, but none had contributed more than Clark. The Giants had won the pennant, thanks to his sneer and his swing.

The Game of My Life
By Will Clark

That was the first time Williams pitched to me in the whole series, and I knew that I would face him sooner or later. He was warming up and I walked over to (hitting coach) Dusty Baker and I asked, "What do you think I ought to look for?" He says, "He's got better control than what they think." I said, "I know that. He's been dealing pretty good this year. I'm going to look for a fastball away," and Dusty said, "That's what I'd look for, too."

His first pitch is a fastball, right on the outside corner. I said, "Oh geez, of all the pitcher's pitches to make, the one I wanted to go get." So I was in a hole, 0-1. Then he threw a fastball up and I fouled it back, 0-2. He missed with a slider. Then he threw three straight fastballs up, and I fouled all of them off. The last one was damn near about head high, way up there, and I was fighting for my life. I wasn't going to give an inch—I was going to hang in here.

Then the next pitch, still 1-2, was a fastball up, the same pitch I had just fouled off the pitch before. For some reason, I don't know how I did it, I got on top of it and hit a line drive back up the middle. Candy Maldonado scored, he was jumping on home plate, and Brett Butler came around and scored. I'm pointing in the dugout, I'm going crazy, (first base coach) Wendell Kim is giving me a hug.

	1	2	3	4	5	6	7	8	9	R	H	E
Cubs	0	0	1	0	0	0	0	0	1	2	10	1
Giants	0	0	0	0	0	0	1	2	x	3	4	1

Clark: 4 at-bats, 1 run, 3 hits, 1 triple, 2 RBIs

The game's conclusion tormented the Cubs and their fans, though Wild Thing defended his approach against Clark.

"There's nothing I can do differently," Williams said. "I'm a fastball pitcher. I come in, that's what I'm going to do. I'm going to throw fastballs. Everybody and their brother knows that. If I go in there thinking, 'Well, I'm going to trick him,' well, that's stupid. I didn't pitch four years in the big leagues just to trick people. I'm not going to change just because it's Will Clark and the bases are loaded.

"I'm not going to sit here and tell you Will Clark got lucky," the pitcher said. "He fouled off some tough pitches to get where we were in the count. And then I threw the ball right down the middle. And then he did what he should have done with it—he whacked it."

Clark shattered playoff records for a five-game series with 13 hits, eight runs, 24 total bases, a 1.200 slugging percentage, and a staggering .650 batting average.

Exhilarated, overjoyed, and soaked in champagne, Clark remembered to share the credit that glorious day. "We just played great the whole time, making all the plays," the Giant said. "My teammates were great and so were Bay Area fans."

In the bedlam of the San Francisco clubhouse, Clark's teammates were in awe.

"This guy is unreal," said Craig. "You saw one of the great performances ever."

"I'm telling you, Will Clark is the best baseball player I've ever seen," agreed catcher Terry Kennedy. "He's the closest thing I've seen to a Ted Williams."

Mitchell put it this way: "Will Clark is not human."

Winning the National League pennant was the crowning achievement of general manager Al Rosen, who took over a last-place club in 1985. It was the highlight of Bob Lurie's 17 years as the team's owner; the lineup card from the decisive game still adorns the wall of his downtown San Francisco office.

The championship was the greatest triumph of most Giants players, too. "There's no doubt about it, when you win and get into the World Series like that, that's as big a stamp as you can put onto something," said Thompson.

Less enjoyable for the Giants was the 1989 World Series they dropped to the Oakland Athletics. The series was interrupted minutes before the start of Game 3 on October 17 by the Loma Prieta Earthquake, which caused at least 63 deaths and more than 3,700 injuries.

"We'd all been through earthquakes before and we didn't think much about it," Clark recalled, "but then we started hearing stories in the dugout about fires in the Marina and the Bay Bridge collapsing, and all of a sudden, we realized that there was something happening that was a lot more important than the World Series."

Clark played for the Giants through the 1993 season, after which he joined the Texas Rangers. In his last seven years, he reached the playoffs three more times, though never again the World Series. The avid hunter announced his retirement in November 2000 from a treetop, with a bow in one hand and a cell phone in the other.

Clark and his wife, Lisa, had a son in the final years of his baseball career, and the parents eventually realized that young Trey is autistic. Since then, Clark has become an advocate and fundraiser for autism research. The family settled in the New Orleans, Louisiana, area.

Clark often visits his old team's new home at 24 Willie Mays Plaza, where he always receives a warm welcome. Writers still ask the Thrill about his glory days when his swing and sneer made the Giants winners. With just a hint of his old intensity—"Oh, Lord! What else? Is that it?"—he accommodates them.

"That single up the middle off Mitch Williams is something I'll never forget," Clark said. "That capped off what was just an unbelievable series. It was a shame one team had to lose, but you know we needed to win."

14

ROBBY THOMPSON

TINY EGO, GIANT HEART

POSITION: second base

SEASONS WITH GIANTS: 1986–1996

ACCOMPLISHMENTS: All-Star in 1988 and 1993; led National League
in triples (11) in 1989; led Giants in runs (73) and hits (149) in 1986;
won Gold Glove and Silver Slugger award in 1993; set Giants career
records for a second baseman with .983 fielding percentage and 873
double plays

GAME OF HIS LIFE: August 22, 1993 versus Florida Marlins

HE WAS A GIANT for 11 years, but there's nothing giant about his ego. Ask
Robby Thompson about his favorite baseball memories, and he's likely to
talk about almost anyone besides himself: Bob Brenly's "awesome" comeback
in his four-error game in 1986 or Don Robinson's dramatic homer in the
1987 playoff race.

"I don't like to remember a lot of stuff that I did," Thompson said. "I like
to remember a lot of stuff that the other guys did. I came up at a great time
with a great group. That's what I remember."

Thompson's modesty can almost make one forget his own innumerable
contributions to San Francisco's cause. But the Giants have been a different
team without their clutch, Gold Glove, All-Star second baseman.

"If the game was on the line, you wanted the ball hit to him, and the hits that he seemed to get were ones that counted," said broadcaster Hank Greenwald.

Thompson broke into the Giants clubhouse suddenly in 1986, jumping from Class AA ball to the big club's starting lineup on the strength of his impressive spring training showing.

"There were rumors it was the worst decision the franchise ever made, but I still have all my minor league options if anybody wants to send me down," Thompson joked. "That's something I'm proud of. I went into spring training every year, whether it was my first year or fifth or tenth or 11th, like I had to win a job. I felt that was my best way to keep it."

Earning all the attention that first spring was Will Clark, the Giants' top draft pick in 1985 and winner of the Golden Spikes Award, college baseball's top honor. Drilling a home run against flamethrower Nolan Ryan in his first major league at-bat, the new first baseman made headlines immediately. To the army of writers surrounding Clark's locker on Opening Day in 1986, the other rookie in San Francisco's lineup was perhaps an afterthought. But Thompson delivered in his debut as well, roping a double off Ryan in the fifth, alertly taking third on a misplay, and later scoring.

"Clark did overshadow him, because of the hype that surrounded him as an award-winner in college," said teammate Mike Krukow. "But that was good for Robby, because it made it easier for him to get comfortable as a big leaguer without dealing with a lot of the limelight. Robby actually had a better year (than Clark) that first year."

San Francisco won 21 more games in 1986 than the year before, and after the season, Thompson was the one honored with The Sporting News Rookie of the Year award.

"Clark was kind of brash, and Robby was more of a steadying influence," Greenwald said. "Both were necessary personalities to that club. They came up together representing the future of the ballclub, and they infused the team with both professionalism and enthusiasm."

Robby Thompson's sure hands and acrobatics helped him break team records for double plays and fielding percentage. *Otto Greule Jr. Getty Images*

The second baseman was part of a core group that helped the Giants win the division in 1987 and the pennant in 1989. But Thompson's greatest year was unquestionably 1993, when he made his second All-Star team, won the Silver Slugger award, and set career highs in home runs, batting average, and RBIs.

"I credit Dusty Baker for helping me with my year in 1993," Thompson said. "He moved me to a heavier bat, and taught me to use the leverage of my long legs and longer arms, and it helped. That's one of the bigger reasons why I had success."

The year marked a new era for the team in many respects. Peter Magowan led a group of investors who bought the team from Bob Lurie, averting the club's relocation to Tampa Bay, Florida. The new owners pushed out manager Roger Craig and promoted Baker, previously the hitting coach, to replace him. The club also signed two-time Most Valuable Player Barry Bonds away from the Pittsburgh Pirates.

"There was an incredible spirit around the team," said broadcaster Ted Robinson. "The franchise was saved when it seemed like it was gone. Barry Bonds arrived and Dusty Baker became the new manager. There was such a breath of fresh air."

San Francisco's 1993 team stands among the all-time greats in Giants history. Thompson, Bonds, third baseman Matt Williams, and catcher Kirt Manwaring would win Gold Gloves. Center fielder Darren Lewis didn't commit an error all year. Starting pitchers John Burkett and Billy Swift each won more than 20 games. Closer Rod Beck saved a team-record 48 contests. And the bats of Thompson, Clark, Williams, and Bonds struck fear in the hearts of pitchers all over the league.

Then boasting power and speed, Bonds amazed all of baseball with both his bat and glove. But Thompson's importance in the lineup wasn't lost on his teammates.

"Robby is one of the most underrated players in the league, but not in this clubhouse," said Swift. "He hits, he turns the double play as well as anyone, and he's a leader."

From the first game, the new Giants tore through their opposition that spring. By the All-Star break, San Francisco had won 59 games against 30 losses, the best record in baseball and nine games ahead of its nearest division rival.

"There's no better lineup in the league," said Bobby Bonds, Barry's father, at the time. Once a Giants star himself, the elder Bonds returned to the club as a hitting coach when his son came to San Francisco. "I'm not surprised by what's happening," he said. "We have a lot of talent. A lot of our young players are just starting to come into their own. They're just beginning to scratch the surface. This offense will only get better."

The season also produced one of the greatest pennant races of all time, as the Atlanta Braves emerged from an early slumber to engage San Francisco in a death sprint to the wire. In the last year before baseball changed from four to six divisions and adopted a wild card in its playoff scheme, Atlanta still played in the seven-team National League West. Once trailing the Giants by ten games, the Braves got hot after acquiring All-Star Fred McGriff from the San Diego Padres on July 18. The first baseman hit .310 for Atlanta and belted 19 home runs in the second half of the season. Though the Giants kept winning, the Braves won even more, taking 49 of their final 65 contests.

"All hell broke loose when 'Crime Dog' went over there," Thompson said of McGriff. "He was a very instrumental part of that season for them."

Atlanta continued the hot pursuit with a come-from-behind win again on August 22, as San Francisco trailed the Florida Marlins at Candlestick Park. In danger of losing more ground to their rivals on the eve of a three-game showdown, the Giants badly needed a jolt to power their pennant drive.

A first-year expansion team, the Marlins led for the majority of the contest. Starting pitcher Pat Rapp held San Francisco scoreless on one hit in the first four innings, retiring Thompson twice on a strikeout and a pop-up. Meanwhile, Florida roughed up Giants ace Burkett for five runs by the seventh inning. Third baseman Gary Sheffield did much of the damage with a home run and three RBIs.

San Francisco scratched out a run in the fifth and scored another in the sixth on a Dave Martinez homer. But the Giants missed a golden opportunity in the seventh when Bonds walked and right fielder Willie McGee doubled to open the inning, yet failed to score as the next three batters struck out. Tough breaks went against the team all day long, from Clark's potential home run that the wind blew into a warning-track fly ball, to Florida center fielder Chuck Carr slipping and flopping on his stomach, yet still managing to catch a Martinez line drive.

In the bottom of the eighth, San Francisco still trailed, 6-2, and the Marlins sensed the rapid approach of "garbage time," the waning moments of a one-sided contest when the final plays become a mere formality. But the Giants weren't ready to throw this one away, and the 31-year-old Thompson got the comeback started with a walk against Florida's Luis Aquino. After Clark and Williams singled to load the bases, Thompson scored on Bonds' sacrifice fly. Then McGee singled to score Clark and Williams, bringing the Giants within a run, 6-5. In the ninth, San Francisco would have a chance.

Marlins closer Bryan Harvey saved 45 games in 1993, no small feat on a young Florida team that only won 64. The All-Star fireman with the mean forkball popped up pinch hitters Todd Benzinger and Mark Carreon to start the inning. Then Martinez managed to coax a walk.

"That kills us, two-out walks," the closer said. "That's how you lose ballgames. Sometimes I get a little too excited with two out, especially with a chance to beat the Giants."

Thompson came to bat, and Harvey threw two quick strikes to the second baseman. Behind in the count, 0-2, Thompson showed nerves of steel in taking a high split-fingered fastball for ball one—a pitch that could have been called strike three. Robinson breathed a sigh of relief after the close call, and focused on putting the ball in play. Harvey threw another split-fingered fastball that caught way too much of the plate. Thompson drilled it and raised his arms in the air as the ball flew toward the left field foul pole. When it cleared the fence, 44,217 fans leaped to their feet and exploded in applause. Down to his last strike, the Giant had turned a 6-5 loss into a 7-6 win with one swing of his bat.

"When Robby Thompson hit the home run that day, I and many others thought the Giants were a team of destiny," said Robinson, who was then working his first year in the Giants radio booth. "It was the most improbable moment in an incredible season. Even though the Marlins were not that good, Bryan Harvey was outstanding. And Robby wasn't a guy who was going to win many games with home runs."

Thompson's teammates stormed out of the dugout to greet him, and Bonds himself carried the delighted second baseman back to the clubhouse.

"My heart is still racing," said a breathless Thompson after the game. "To win in the last inning like that, and knowing it's a big ballgame. . . . you can't always be cool and collected. We showed a little emotion and it felt great."

The Game of My Life
By Robby Thompson

Bryan Harvey was known for his split-finger pitch. He was in the elite of closers at that time, well-respected by his peers and his opponents and the umpires. With two strikes, Harvey threw a split that was borderline. It could have been a strike, and maybe should have been, who knows? It was one of those pitches that crosses the plate, and you say, "Oh my God, was that the end of my at-bat?" If it had been called a strike, I would have had no argument with it. But I took it and got the call and got new life. It forced him to throw another pitch.

He threw the split again and hung it and I hit the home run. I got lucky. This game's all about luck. You've got to have some ability, but it's better to be lucky than good.

The home run means a lot only because it was a big win for us. Any time you do something individually like that, like win the game with a walk-off home run, and Barry Bonds is the first guy there to hug you, and the rest of the team is mobbing you, and it's a meaningful game in a pennant race, sure, it means a lot.

Though if we had won the division and moved on, it would have a lot more meaning to it. Any time you win 103 games, you should go to the playoffs.

	1	2	3		4	5	6		7	8	9		R	H	E
Marlins	0	0	0		1	0	2		2	1	0		6	12	0
Giants	0	0	0		0	1	1		0	3	2		7	10	1

Thompson: 3 at-bats, 2 runs, 1 hit, 1 HR, 2 RBIs, 2 walks

If the Giants were thankful for Thompson's blast when he hit it, they were even more grateful three days later when the relentless Braves completed a three-game sweep at Candlestick. Atlanta pulled within four and a half games, and but for Thompson's monster August numbers—his .394 batting average and eight homers led the team—the fierce pennant race would have been even tighter.

An agonizing eight-game losing streak in September cost San Francisco the lead, and with two weeks to play, suddenly the Giants had to overcome a four-game deficit. Incredibly, they did, winning ten of 11 games and tying the Braves before the final weekend. But during this hot streak, the Giants lost their star second baseman. Trevor Hoffman, then a rookie in the San Diego Padres bullpen, hit Thompson in the face with a fastball on September 24. No one ever suggested Hoffman threw at him deliberately, but the impact fractured Thompson's left cheekbone and left his quick return to the lineup doubtful at best.

"It hurt. It hurt a lot," he said. "I remember the ambulance ride. It was the worst ride I ever had in my life. Actually I was lucky there wasn't more damage. After a 96-mph fastball on the cheekbone, you'd expect worse."

San Francisco could ill afford his loss. The Giants had already lost significant playing time from injured key players like Clark, Lewis, and pitcher Trevor Wilson, while the Braves were mostly injury-free. In response to the team's crippled state, Bonds fed the press a salacious quote. "We've got shotguns and they've got Uzis," the left fielder said. "That just means we can't afford to miss."

Atlanta played its final games with the Colorado Rockies and swept the series against the expansion club. To the lasting dismay of the Giants and their fans, Colorado failed to beat the Braves a single time in 13 contests that year.

San Francisco finished the year at Dodger Stadium, needing wins in each of the last four games to force a tiebreaker against the Braves. A heavy dose of Bonds-powered offense helped the Giants win the first three.

Thompson made a dramatic return to play in the October 3 finale, wearing a transparent plastic face shield to protect his healing cheekbone from further trauma.

"It was very important to me to get back. I didn't want it any other way," he said. "One, we were going for the pennant there, and two, I wanted to get back and face live pitching. I didn't want to go a whole off-season without getting another at-bat."

However, the game was a disaster for San Francisco. Baker sent the promising rookie Salomon Torres out to pitch, and Los Angeles roughed him up for three runs in the first four innings. The bullpen fared even worse, and the Giants offense got nowhere against Dodgers pitcher Kevin Gross, who threw a complete game.

The 12-1 stomping was a crushing disappointment. With 103 wins, San Francisco finished second and failed to reach the playoffs, becoming one of the greatest near-misses in baseball history. No other club won so many games without advancing to the postseason in the 25 years that baseball employed a four-team playoff format. Since the eight-team playoffs began in 1995, clubs have won divisions with as few as 82 wins.

"I just wish there was a wild card back then," Thompson said. "We might have won everything. We had a hell of a club."

Just a year after the team nearly left San Francisco, the thrilling race full of comeback wins and drama electrified Bay Area fans.

"I was down when we got beat, but that lasted for about five minutes," said Baker. "Then I thought about the season and all we accomplished. I'll never forget it."

Thompson patrolled second base for San Francisco through 1996 before retiring at age 34. Neither he nor the Giants matched their 1993 success in his final seasons, but Thompson took on a new role in his later years. The rookie kid had become a learned mentor who showed his younger teammates how to make it in the bigs. "Robby Thompson basically saved my career," said shortstop Royce Clayton, a Giants regular from 1992 to 1995, who credits his teammate with teaching him how to turn the double play. "He took me under his wing and taught me how to be a professional on and off the field. From a great veteran like Robby, it meant the world to me. I thank God for having him around early in my career."

To the Giant who learned the ropes from teammates like Krukow, Brenly, Jeffrey Leonard and Chili Davis, there was simply no other choice, Thompson said. "I think it's every veteran's job to help out and to pass on whatever you can to the younger players coming up, whether they're fighting for your job or not," he said.

After 1993, several injuries contributed to a decline in Thompson's performance and playing time; he never played in as many as 100 games again.

"I would have loved to play more," Thompson said. "It all took a toll on my body. With my shoulder surgeries, my knee, my back, and this and that, it was time to go. In '96 I tore my hip flexor muscle. There was one thing after another.

"But I got the most out of my body," he said. "I'd do it all the same way again. I could always look at myself in the mirror. I lasted 11 years and I'm proud to say I spent 'em all with the San Francisco Giants."

Thompson coached at first base for the Giants in 2000 and 2001 before taking a coaching job with the Cleveland Indians in 2002. The move brought him closer to his family in Tequesta, Florida, especially during the Indians' spring training in nearby Winter Haven. He hopes one day to manage and expects to always stay in baseball. "I'll be in it for the rest of my life," he said.

In San Francisco, his name can still be found all over the Giants record book. Thompson broke franchise career records for a second baseman with his .983 fielding percentage and 873 double plays. He leads all second basemen in the San Francisco era with 11 consecutive Opening Day starts, and he set records for the most games, putouts, and assists. Proud of his work with the leather, he contributed steadily with his lumber, too, hitting .257 for his career while smacking 119 home runs and 238 doubles.

How did he do it? True to form, Thompson points to others: teammates, coaches, managers, and general managers—anybody who helped him, anybody but himself. His wife, Brenda, gets his highest praise. Sweethearts since they were both 11, Robby and Brenda have four children.

"She has been the greatest inspiration ever," he said. "I could not have done it without her. It wasn't easy with the kids when I was playing and on the road so much. She was then and is now the rock and backbone of the family, the glue for my whole career."

Only when gently pushed and cajoled will the ever-modest Thompson give himself any credit for his remarkable success. "I credit myself with pure determination to reach the big league level and not letting anything stand in my way," he said. "Getting there I proved a lot of people wrong, and staying there I proved even more people wrong, and I made a great living for my family."

He may not seek attention, but on rare occasions, Thompson permits himself to enjoy it, like he did on September 30, 1999, the day of the Giants' last game at Candlestick. The Dodgers won that afternoon, but the special event came afterwards, when dozens of Giants from the park's 40-year history returned to the field to "tell it goodbye." The crowd greeted Thompson affectionately, chanting, "Rob-by! Rob-by!" No one drew a warmer response.

"I'll never forget the last time I walked out on the grass at Candlestick, when they brought all the guys back, and introduced me and the "Rob-by" chant went on forever and ever and ever," he said. "Duane Kuiper was out there at second base with me, and he pats me in the ass and says, 'Enjoy it.'"

With tears in his eyes, Thompson did just that.

15

DARREN LEWIS

"NO HITS OUT HERE"

POSITION: center field

SEASONS WITH GIANTS: 1991–1995

ACCOMPLISHMENTS: set major league record with 392 consecutive errorless games from 1990-1994; led National League in triples (9) in 1994; led Giants in stolen bases in 1992 (28), 1993 (46), and 1994 (30); won Gold Glove in 1994

GAME OF HIS LIFE: July 24, 1994 versus New York Mets

WHEN DARREN LEWIS PLAYED for San Francisco, the brazen center fielder with the magic glove risked a game that few ballplayers would dare: he talked trash to his older teammate, Barry Bonds.

"Take the day off today, Barry. I got everything," Lewis once told him.

"You cocky little kid," Bonds scoffed.

But "D-Lew" turned the famous left fielder into a believer. For five years with San Francisco, the speedster chased down balls that often appeared uncatchable, none more so than the screamer he caught on July 24, 1994.

The Giants led the New York Mets, 3-0, on a Sunday afternoon at Shea Stadium. Lewis and Bonds had fueled a rally in the first to give San Francisco the lead, and starting pitcher Bud Black had mowed down six straight Mets to nicely start the game. Leading off the bottom of the third, New York center fielder Ryan Thompson drilled Black's pitch deep to left-center, and to everyone in the park but Lewis, the ball looked way gone. The 26-year-old Giant sprinted toward the fence, leaped up high against it and flung his arm as high as he could over it. His glove arm slammed down against the wall's back side. D-Lew fell back to the turf and regained his balance. Then he jumped about wildly in jubilation.

Only then did the 32,940 breathless spectators realize that they'd been robbed. Lewis flung the ball into the stands and an incredulous Bonds congratulated the euphoric center fielder.

"I couldn't believe he caught it," said Bonds. "The best part was when he came down and said to me, 'There's no hits out here, B! None!'"

Thompson had trotted almost to second base before he saw his misfortune. He waved a finger at Lewis and turned toward the dugout, shaking his head in disbelief. For Lewis, the play was especially sweet because it was his first home run theft in the majors and it came just two days after a disappointing near-miss.

"Jeff Kent had hit a ball in almost the same spot," he said. "I was playing Kent in the same place as Ryan Thompson. It was the same identical play but then I missed the ball by about two feet."

Lewis made a career out of not just turning great plays, but also making routine ones more frequently than any of his rivals. In fact, the center fielder shattered a major league record by playing 392 errorless games from his debut in 1990 until midseason in 1994. The previous record held by Phillies and Tigers outfielder Don Demeter was 267 games, the equivalent of five months shorter.

"Offensively, I was an average player. I hit .250 and stole quite a few bases for the time that I played (247 in 13 seasons)," he said. "For a guy who was a singles hitter, I drove in quite a few runs (342). But I was recognized more as a defensive player."

The Gold Glove winner in 1994 takes pride in the streak and even more in the work that produced it. "I was always prepared, I was never taken by surprise and I always worked at my craft," Lewis said. "I took

Darren Lewis followed up his record-breaking errorless streak with a remarkable catch in the game of his life to prevent a home run. *Brace Photo*

fly balls every day and I went to scouting meetings. I had consistent focus on each play in throwing to the right bases. I looked at the tendencies of hitters, in accordance with who was pitching. I put my time in and I loved doing it.

"That's the reason that record happened," he said. "I never took one pitch off when I played defense. I never looked into the stands or took a break. I spent the majority of my career on a winning team, and when I look back on it, I think one of the reasons is that when you have a center fielder with Gold Glove defensive capability, it makes your team and your pitching staff much better."

Bonds put it more simply: "He made a lot of catches that saved the pitcher's life."

After witnessing his teammate's acrobatics against the Mets, the grateful pitcher Black would certainly agree. "I've been around 13 years, and that might be the best I've ever seen," said Black. "I wish I could say I planned it. That would have been a good time to just walk off the field."

New York struck back in the seventh and briefly took the lead after catcher Todd Hundley homered against Giants reliever Rich Monteleone. But San Francisco answered with a three-run rally in the eighth, powered by the bats of Bonds and Matt Williams. The newly acquired Darryl Strawberry contributed a hit and an RBI, and closer Rod Beck retired the last four Mets to earn his 23rd save.

D-Lew had a good game even besides his highlight reel catch. Against Mets starter Bobby Jones, the center fielder walked, stole a base, and scored in the first: doubled in the second; and walked again in the sixth.

"He had a big overhand curveball and he was always around the plate," recalled Lewis. "For some reason, I could pick the ball up well against him."

But robbing Patterson in the third was Lewis' favorite contribution in a close contest that the Giants won, 8-6. A photographer captured the play in a sequence of seven shots. Today the framed set hangs from Lewis' office wall, visual proof that at least in baseball, crime still pays.

The Game of My Life
By Darren Lewis

Boom! Thompson hit a bomb. I ran a long way to catch it, to the left field side of second base, deep. I timed the whole play. When I jumped up, I could see it when I was over the fence. It was in my glove. I was so excited that (upon landing) I had to jump up and down. I had to go crazy. Barry was standing right next to me. We talked a little stuff and I threw the ball back.

Thompson was standing about five or six steps from second base. He just pointed at me to say, "Okay, I owe you one, I'll remember that."

I had made a couple of catches like that at Cal Berkeley and U.C. Santa Barbara, but I had always dreamed about doing it in the major leagues. To rob somebody's home run, it's a play that you may not get all year.

That was my favorite catch. I ended up going on to make a lot of catches like that, but that was the best one because I ran so far, jumped super-high over the fence and caught it.

I felt that was the defining moment of my career. I was always trying to make plays like that and help out my pitchers.

	1	2	3	4	5	6	7	8	9	R	H	E
Giants	2	1	0	0	2	0	0	3	0	8	12	1
Mets	0	0	0	2	1	0	3	0	0	6	8	1

Lewis: 3 at-bats, 1 hit, 1 run, 2 walks, 1 stolen base

Lewis stole his 30th base to take the team lead from Bonds on August 10 of that year. Likewise, the 1994 Giants were just starting to get hot when the show suddenly came to an end. A salary cap proposed by team owners led to a players strike that ended the season and cancelled the World Series for the first time in 90 years.

"We all went home just dazed and confused," said Lewis. "If you look at the standings, we were just three games out. That's when we were really starting to pick things up. We just got Darryl Strawberry. With him in the lineup behind Barry and Matt Williams, we were on our way to something special. We just ran out of time."

Lewis didn't know it yet, but his San Francisco days were numbered, too, after baseball restarted in 1995. The team traded him to the Cincinnati Reds on July 21 in the deal that made Deion Sanders a Giant for half a year. It was one of many changes the Peter Magowan-led ownership group made in its first few seasons.

"After '93, Will Clark left, Darren was traded, and I was traded in '95. The whole team took on a new face," said former Giants shortstop Royce Clayton. "I think when you look back, the ownership wanted to put their stamp on it and Barry was their stamp. The rest of us were part of that old regime that had nothing to do with the new regime."

Lewis also played for the White Sox, Dodgers, Red Sox, and Cubs, reaching the playoffs three times before retiring in 2002. He settled in San Ramon and puts his expertise to work as a Giants minor league instructor of outfielders and base running. Later Lewis began coaching the Dougherty Valley High School baseball team that included his son, Austin.

Lewis also co-founded Tastes on the Fly, a successful chain of airport restaurants in San Francisco, New York and Boston. Then he completed a bachelors degree in interdisciplinary studies at UC Berkeley, writing a thesis about the globalization of baseball that became part of the Hall of Fame library.

"It took me a year but I got an A on it," he said. "Getting my diploma felt great, and it's especially good for my son to see that his old man has his degree and is more than just a ballplayer."

16

KIRK RUETER

WOODY'S WONDER

POSITION: pitcher

SEASONS WITH GIANTS: 1996–2005

ACCOMPLISHMENTS: led Giants in wins (16) in 1998; led Giants in ERA (3.23) in 2002; leads all left-handed San Francisco pitchers in games started (277) and wins (105)

GAME OF HIS LIFE: September 17, 1997 versus Los Angeles Dodgers

---

GIANTS FANS REMEMBER KIRK RUETER for his 105 wins, his contagious smile, and the popular nickname by which he's widely known. "Woody" likes to remember San Francisco fans for their wild, rabid support during the must-win game of September 17, 1997.

"I saw all around the upper deck, thousands of fans chanting, 'Beat LA,'" Rueter said. "That was the first feel I got of the Giants-Dodgers rivalry and my first taste of a September playoff run."

After last-place finishes in 1995 and 1996, the Giants took bold action prior to the 1997 campaign. New general manager Brian Sabean made wholesale roster changes, releasing the popular second baseman Robby Thompson, trading away slugger Matt Williams, and bringing aboard such new talent as Jeff Kent and J.T. Snow. The remodeled team became a consistent winner for the next eight years, but at the time, the Bay Area howled at the loss of its stars. One fan went so far as to publicly "divorce" the club, shipping his Giants hats, shirts, and baseball cards to the team office. Writers castigated the general manager. "I am not an idiot," Sabean famously shot back.

"I got traded over in '96. Sabes did a lot of dealing," said Rueter. "He brought in Jeff Kent, J.T. Snow, Jose Vizcaino, all new guys that were out to prove something. We got off to a hot start and carried it through the year."

Picked by many to finish last again, San Francisco streaked to nine straight wins in April and won 13 of their first 16 games, the best in baseball. The Giants clawed and fought to hold a narrow lead in the National League West all year until a critical four-game losing streak allowed Los Angeles to pass them by. The Dodgers led the division by two games when they arrived in San Francisco for a crucial series starting September 17. Los Angeles started Chan Ho Park in the first contest. The Giants gave the ball to Rueter.

"Rueter was awesome for us that year," recalled Giants shortstop Jose Vizcaino. "Every time we needed a big win, he was the guy we always wanted to get on the mound. He came through when we needed it."

At risk of falling three games behind with ten left in the season, San Francisco could hardly have needed this one more. The game was the most exciting and hard-fought contest that Candlestick had seen in years. Home attendance had disappointed the club for much of the season, but 56,625 fans filled the park to ferociously demand a win. In this electric atmosphere, Rueter set to work against a potent Los Angeles offense. Woody shut down the Dodgers quickly in the first, retiring speedsters Eric Young and Otis Nixon and hard-hitting catcher Mike Piazza in order.

In the home half, the Giants pleased their crowd when Darryl Hamilton coaxed a walk ahead of Barry Bonds. Park missed with his first two pitches to the slugger, and then challenged him with a heater across the plate. It proved a costly mistake, as Bonds blasted the ball into the upper deck in right. Screaming fans went berserk as the Giants took a 2-0 lead.

"I couldn't believe he tried to challenge Barry in that situation," said Darren Lewis, a former Giant who played left field for Los Angeles that night.

Kirk Rueter handcuffed the Dodgers in a must-win contest before a raucous crowd on September 17, 1997. *Brace Photo*

To further aggravate his rivals, Bonds stood to admire his shot, walked two steps and then twirled in a 360 before starting his home run trot.

"When you're Barry, you can do those things. You really have to bite your lip a little bit," said Piazza.

"Barry got everybody amped when he hit that homer," Rueter said. "When he did a little pirouette, he gave everybody a little sense of confidence."

Rueter, then 26 and pitching in his fifth big league season, threw an 86-mph fastball, slower than the change-ups of some opposing pitchers. But the southpaw with a tricky breaking ball outlasted and outperformed countless power pitchers. On this night, Woody was masterful, holding the Dodgers hitless for the first four innings.

"I couldn't just blow people away. I had to pitch to corners and change speeds and let my defense play behind me. I pitched the same way I'd pitched my whole life," Rueter said. "I knew it would be a game that required concentration, like any game at this stage. But I didn't have any problems with my emotions, maybe because I don't throw hard enough to overthrow."

Perhaps taking extra motivation from Bonds' showboating, Park began a tear of his own. Following the home run, Park paralyzed the Giants offense for the next six innings, retiring 17 of the next 19 batters he faced. Los Angeles tagged the Giants for a run in the fifth when right fielder Raul Mondesi launched Rueter's second pitch high and deep to left. Bonds didn't even look at the ball that easily cleared the old Candlestick bleachers. The Dodgers' first hit produced their first run, cutting San Francisco's lead in half.

"Mondesi," Rueter recalled, "always gave me fits."

But Woody shook off the setback and resumed his systematic frustration of the Dodgers lineup. He struck out Eric Karros on a sinker to end a threat in the sixth, roaring with the crowd as he trotted back to the dugout. After Mondesi walked to lead off the seventh, Rueter used his sinker again to get a ground ball from the Dodgers' Todd Zeile. Then the pitcher himself smoothly fielded the ball and started a rally-crushing double play.

"He threw it good," said Piazza. "He worked fast, kept the ball down, and changed speeds. He was a crafty lefty."

When Rueter jogged off the mound for the last time, the spectators rewarded him with a standing ovation, and the Giants weren't the only ones who heard it. Their blue-clad visitors couldn't help but notice the fierce mob screaming for their blood.

"I'll never forget that night. The crowd was vicious," said the Dodgers' Lewis. "There were hecklers in the left-field bleachers throwing pennies and peanuts at me all game."

Candlestick Park holds few advantages over its successor at 24 Willie Mays Plaza, but one must admit this about the chilly stadium: the motley crew that inhabited it was less prone to cell phone distractions and more inclined to torment the Giants' opponents.

"They were screaming at me, 'You're not a Giant anymore.' 'You can't hit.' 'You suck,'" Lewis said. "You name it, I heard it. I was disappointed in them."

San Francisco never scored again, but Roberto Hernandez, acquired at the trade deadline that season, made Woody's performance stand up with a stifling two-inning save. In relief of Woody, Hernandez warmed up a cold Candlestick night with 100-mph heat, striking out two and allowing only a walk to the seven batters he faced. The last of them was Zeile, who rolled a weak ground ball to shortstop. Vizcaino picked it up and fired to Snow at first.

The ballgame was over, but the cheering fans lingered long after, savoring the win that saved the Giants' season for at least another day.

The Game of My Life
By Kirk Rueter

That was a big game to pitch in. I got excited to pitch every game, because I love to compete and I love to win. I'd even get nervous in spring training games. It helped me to treat it as any other game, to try to go out and do the things I'd done that whole season. But when I walked out the tunnel and 60,000 people were screaming, it got my adrenaline going more than a spring training game did. I calmed down and got into it. I was able to make my pitches when I had to.

I knew I had to keep Young and Nixon off base because they run on you like crazy. Getting them out ahead of Karros, Piazza, and Zeile was one of the big things. There was one time when they both got on, which was just what I was trying not to do. That was the big inning, because if they scored a couple and took the lead, things might have turned out differently. So when I struck out Karros, I got a little more animated than I usually was.

Everybody on that team had struggled somewhere in their career. Everybody (came from) an organization that had given up on them or traded them. I don't think a lot of people gave us much of a chance to finish even in the middle of the pack. That's what made it such a magical year. It's a lot more fun when nobody thinks you can do it and you prove everybody wrong.

	1	2	3	4	5	6	7	8	9	R	H	E
Dodgers	0	0	0	0	1	0	0	0	0	1	4	2
Giants	2	0	0	0	0	0	0	0	x	2	3	0

Rueter: win, 7 innings pitched, 4 hits, 1 run, 1 walk, 4 strikeouts

---

When Woody's Giants visited St. Louis, the team often stopped by "The Shed" at Rueter's home in Nashville, Illinois. Full of arcade games and sports memorabilia, the 4,500-square-foot recreation center about an hour from Busch Stadium provided a nice diversion when the club played the Cardinals.

Rueter began spending more time at home when he retired in 2006 at age 35. "I'm being a husband and a dad a little better than I was in the past," he said. "I want to watch my girls grow up and be around when they need me."

But the Giant has plenty of reminders of his big league days around him. The Shed is chock full of bats, balls, jerseys, trophies and baseball pictures. There's the team's parting gift to him, an enormous Woody bobblehead that's even bigger than the real Rueter. Plus, his hometown friends far from San Francisco have picked up his baseball moniker. Woody's teammates bestowed the nickname because of his uncanny resemblance to the animated wooden cowboy in the 1995 film, Toy Story. "Even the people back here call me that. I don't think I'm ever going to shake it," he said.

During his ten years with the Giants, Rueter reached the playoffs four times, played in the World Series, and won more games than any other San Francisco lefty.

"I miss the fifth day," said the southpaw. "The other four days, I don't miss as much."

———————

Rueter's gritty win on September 17, 1997 actually proved a template for his many years of success. As he did his entire career, the shrewd pitcher with the mid-80s fastball worked the corners, kept batters off-balance, and left his defeated opponents shaking their heads in frustration.

"Frankly, with Rueter, you come away from the game wondering why you didn't get three hits, wondering why you wound up with an 0-fer," said Zeile, who finished the game 0-for-three. "But that's the sign of a real good pitcher."

High fives and hugs marked a warm but subdued celebration. A dogpile on the diamond wouldn't do; there was a rematch the next day. But there was no overstating the game's drama or its importance to San Francisco.

"If you didn't like baseball before tonight, you have to after tonight," said Baker. "This is what baseball is all about. This is the only time I wish I could still play."

"This is the one we needed," said the manager. "It was the one we badly wanted. It starts with your starting pitcher, and Kirk Rueter was outstanding tonight."

Yet Woody's wonder would have meant little without another win to follow it. San Francisco needed to sweep the series to catch Los Angeles before the season's final week. High stakes, excitement, clutch hitting, and fearless pitching returned to the diamond, but the sequel was a very different game. And the pitcher it starred was a very different Giant.

17

ROD BECK

"THIS IS WHO I AM"

POSITION: pitcher

SEASONS WITH GIANTS: 1991–1997

ACCOMPLISHMENTS: All-Star in 1993, 1994, and 1997; set Giants single-season record in saves (48) in 1993; set Giants career record with 199 saves

GAME OF HIS LIFE: September 18, 1997 versus Los Angeles Dodgers

---

BEFORE THE START OF the Candlestick epic of September 18, 1997, an eight-year-old girl behind the San Francisco dugout called out to manager Dusty Baker.

"Dusty, can I talk to you?" asked the young Giants fan. When Baker turned to speak to her, the little girl begged the skipper: "Dusty, whatever happens today, whatever you do, don't put in Rod Beck!"

One could understand why Beck believed he deserved greater respect. The Giants had counted on him to nail down their wins for five years, and the long-haired closer with the menacing scowl had rarely let them down. A three-time All-Star, Beck had demolished franchise records with 199 saves in his career and 48 in a single season. Along the way, "Shooter" twice set National League records for consecutive saves without a misfire.

But the portly pitcher had fallen into a most untimely slump. As his arm tired and his heater slowed, the league began to hit Beck hard, and just three days earlier, he suffered a horrific and costly loss. In that game, San Francisco was close enough to taste a rare win against Atlanta, leading the Braves in the ninth inning, 4-1. Beck had a perfect chance to save his 200th career game. Then three Atlanta singles set the stage for Fred McGriff, and "Crime Dog" creamed Beck's splitter for a two-run game-winning homer. The heartbreaking defeat knocked the Giants out of first place. To many fans, the just-acquired Roberto Hernandez seemed a better choice to close.

"Beck had a great first half for us, but his workload was huge," shortstop Rich Aurilia said. "In the second half, he started to wear down. That's why they made the trade to get Hernandez and Danny Darwin."

When Baker summoned Hernandez to finish a tooth-and-nail game on September 17, it appeared Beck had lost his position as the closer of the team. But Shooter's moment to shine arrived the next day in the slugfest against the Dodgers. The Giant wouldn't earn a save in the game, but he saved San Francisco's season nonetheless.

"Without a doubt, it was a must-win game for us," said Beck. "Out of all the series we played in the course of the year, that was the one we had to have."

Los Angeles drew blood in the first inning when Otis Nixon homered off southpaw Terry Mulholland. The ball cleared the fence just inches over the glove of left fielder Barry Bonds. The Giants struck right back in the bottom half when a hustling Bonds tripled off Tom Candiotti. Moments later, the Dodgers pitcher threw a hanging curve to Glenallen Hill, and the right fielder knocked it up the middle, scoring Bonds to tie the game.

Both teams threatened in the next innings, but the pitchers shut down each budding rally. When Dodgers batters led off with hits in the second and third, Mulholland got the following hitters to ground into double plays both times. Los Angeles returned the favor after San Francisco's Bill Mueller cracked a single in the third. Bonds hit a bullet to first, and the Dodgers turned a sharp twin killing.

The tie broke in the fourth on a solo homer by J.T. Snow. A first-year Giant enjoying his finest offensive season, Snow worked the count full before

Rod Beck saved the Giants' playoff hopes with a masterful escape against the Dodgers on September 18, 1997. *Brace Photo*

drilling a 77-mph curveball. San Francisco then pushed its advantage in the fifth when Darryl Hamilton and Mueller singled ahead of Bonds. The slugger belted out a 70-mph knuckler to give the Giants a 5-1 lead.

In the sixth, Nixon reached first on a rare error by the Giants first baseman. The speedster bunted to Snow and knocked the ball loose from his glove as he ran by. Nixon advanced to second on a wild pitch and scored on an Eric Karros single to center. Then Karros scored on Todd Zeile's double, and Los Angeles closed the gap to 5-3. The Dodgers struck again in the seventh against new San Francisco pitcher Julian Tavarez. Todd Hollandsworth and Eric Young singled ahead of Mike Piazza. Baker summoned Hernandez to face the All-Star catcher, and Piazza ripped a two-out hit to knock both runners home.

After seven frames, the crucial game was tied, 5-5. The bullpens kept it that way in scoreless eighth and ninth innings. Finally entering in the tenth was Beck, then 29 years old, the fifth Giants pitcher of the day. The appearance could have hardly started worse for the beleaguered closer. Beck got ahead of Piazza, 1-2, and threw a splitter low and off the plate. Piazza dug it out and blooped a single to right, to the uneasy crowd's dismay. Grumbling increased when Karros followed with a single on the left field line. After Raul Mondesi hit another single, Los Angeles had loaded the bases with no one out.

A nightmare was unfolding, and San Francisco's season hung by a thread. In full revolt, fans booed loud and hard enough to knock a thinner pitcher off the mound. It was hardly fitting treatment for the best closer the Giants had ever had, and it upset many players wearing orange and black that day.

"They were booing to the point where they wanted Beck off the field," said teammate Marvin Benard. "I think if he could have choked anybody and everybody in the stands, he would have. What kept him going was that his teammates were still behind him."

As grim as the situation looked to the Giants and their fans, they were actually very lucky that the game was still tied. Anyone but a catcher would

140

have scored from second on Mondesi's single. Piazza still remembers the play.

"I should have scored," Piazza said. "It was a line drive to right, with no outs, and the third base coach held me up, which may or may not have been the right move. On the road, you really should go for the win there. But I'd caught 140 games that year and I was pretty gassed."

Baker slowly walked to the mound, while San Francisco southpaw Rich Rodriguez warmed up. Fans sarcastically cheered the move they expected the skipper to make.

"Of course, I wasn't sure what he was going to do," Beck recalled. "But the way he was walking, I was pretty sure he was going to leave me in. That showed a lot of confidence."

Indeed, Baker had no intention of pulling his star pitcher. "Dig deep" was the simple message he delivered. "I told him, 'Hey man, whatever you've learned over your career, break it out right now,'" the manager said.

Baker didn't tell Shooter about the little girl's urgent pregame plea, but the skipper thought about her as he walked back to the dugout. "Come on Rodney," Baker said to himself, "you've gotta get out of this or this little girl is gonna hate me for life."

Next up was Zeile, who already had two hits and a RBI. Chewing hard on his gum, the closer glared in and rocked his pitching arm in his trademark pendulum swing.

"There was no time for doubt. I had to find a way to get out of it," Beck said. "One run was not an option. I felt if I gave up one run, I might as well give them all. I just knew I had to get them out."

With two strikes, Beck fired Zeile a 94-mph fastball knee high on the inside corner. The third baseman didn't even swing at the fastest heater Beck had thrown all year. The umpire rung up Zeile with an emphatic called strike three. The first out of the frame was huge, though more trouble loomed on deck.

Eddie Murray pinch-hit in the Dodgers pitcher's slot. "Steady Eddie" hit better than .400 lifetime with the bases loaded. Scouting reports said Murray was a first-pitch fastball hitter, leading Beck to decide on a simple strategy: "junkball him until I got him where I wanted."

Shooter threw a first-pitch splitter to the future Hall of Famer, and Murray knocked an easy chopper straight to Jeff Kent. The second baseman shot home—over a ducking Beck—for a force out on Piazza, and then catcher Brian Johnson fired to a reaching Snow to just beat the 41-year-old Murray to first. The unusual double play crushed the Los Angeles scoring threat. Against all odds, Beck had brought San Francisco back from almost certain death.

"That's my single most thrilling moment in nine years behind the mic with the Giants," said broadcaster Ted Robinson. "Before the Rod Beck escape, it appeared the game was done. That he got out of that inning was the most incredulous thing. That's when I started to think that they would actually win the game."

Beck clapped his hands and screamed as he marched back to the bench. Baker spun to face the crowd and swung his arms like mad. The fans leaped to their feet to wildly cheer their closer once more. "All of a sudden, he was everybody's best friend again," Aurilia said. "All 50,000 people were cheering and going nuts."

Beck pitched two more scoreless frames without allowing another hit or walk. The three-inning outing was his longest in five years.

The Giants failed to score in the tenth or eleventh frames. After Bonds' homer in the fifth, the Dodgers walked the slugger three straight times. Someone else would have to beat Los Angeles this afternoon. Enter the catcher, Johnson, leading off the bottom of the twelfth. New Dodgers hurler Mark Guthrie threw him only one pitch, and Johnson smashed the heater just over the left-field fence. In an instant, the barnburner game came to a spectacular end. San Francisco defeated its arch enemy, 6-5.

Blasting over the standing crowd's earsplitting roar was the Giants fight song: "When the Giants come to town, it's bye bye baby. Every time the chips are down, it's bye bye baby."

Rarely had the words seemed more appropriate. Instead of suffering a season-dooming loss, San Francisco had tied Los Angeles for first place with nine games to play.

Johnson pumped both arms in triumph as he trotted around the bags. Beck joined a frenzied Giants mob that swarmed him on the field. Bonds lifted Baker off his feet in the delirious gala. Screaming fans waved brooms in celebration of the two-game series sweep.

"Oh man, I'm so happy, I don't know what to do," said Baker. "I'm so happy for Brian, a local dude who came home. This is something he'll talk about for years to come. This is the best thing I've ever seen since I've been in baseball."

Johnson's homer lives forever in San Francisco's highlight reels. In years to come, life-sized photos of his moment adorned the walls at Candlestick. Less celebrated is the gutsy fireman who slammed the door on defeat. But Beck made the victory possible by retiring eight Dodgers in a row. In the clubhouse, a writer asked Shooter to describe his emotions in the rags-to-riches game. Beck wouldn't even try. "I don't think you could duplicate 'em for the world," the pitcher said.

The Game of My Life
By Rod Beck

The fans didn't want me in the game. There were a lot of bad things going on for me at that time. We had just got Roberto Hernandez and there was a perception of me losing my job to him. I knew I was coming down to the wire of my last season in a Giants uniform. It was a great game, don't get me wrong. But it's kind of good and bad in my memory bank.

The three base hits weren't hit real hard. I felt I was throwing the ball pretty good. But nothing was going my way. I remember the bases were loaded with nobody out. The fans were letting me have it, and they started applauding when Dusty came out to the mound. Then the crowd started booing Dusty for letting me stay in. When you spend your whole career in one uniform, and you know you're leaving, it's hard to think that nobody wants you.

I threw breaking balls to Zeile to get ahead in the count. Then I got him looking on a fastball on the inside part of the plate. I wasn't throwing real hard anymore. It was a very hittable pitch, had he looked for it. Then Murray hit the ground ball for the double play, second to home to first.

I was pretty upset with the fans but I don't like to come off that way. It was the one moment in time when I felt like that. For me, it was not so much an "I told you so" as it was "This is where I should be, this is who I am" to the city of San Francisco. I'm very grateful for the time that I spent there.

I'll never forget it, but for different reasons than the fans and Dusty and a lot of other people.

	1	2	3	4	5	6	7	8	9	10	11	12	R	H	E
Dodgers	1	0	0	0	0	2	2	0	0	0	0	0	5	15	1
Giants	1	0	0	1	3	0	0	0	0	0	0	1	6	12	1

Beck: win, 3 innings pitched, 3 hits, 0 runs, 0 walks, 2 strikeouts

---

Another ten days remained in the 1997 season, though the Giants seemed to win the National League West on September 18.

"That's when we really got the feeling that this was our time," said Kirk Rueter, winning pitcher of the night before. "We knew we were gonna win, that we were supposed to win."

They didn't admit it yet, but the two one-run losses left the Dodgers crushed. They left town in a tie but hopelessly behind in confidence and momentum.

"It was a frustrating series for us," Piazza said. "Those games really knocked the wind out of our sails."

On September 27, against the Padres at Candlestick, Beck struck out San Diego's Greg Vaughn to clinch the division title for San Francisco. But the pitcher's suspicions about his future proved correct. After the season, the Giants acquired Robb Nen and let their longtime closer walk.

"I loved having Shooter on the team. He did whatever it took to win," said Baker. "It's not easy to take, but you realize things are going to change. He's still one of my favorite dudes of all time."

Beck earned his 200th save in a Cubs uniform. He saved a career-best 51 contests for Chicago in 1998.

"I didn't want to leave (San Francisco). It was very difficult," Beck said. "The money was fine. All I wanted was another year on the contract. I wanted to pitch in the new ballpark and I felt I deserved that, but they wouldn't guarantee the third year.

"Without a doubt, God works in mysterious ways," Beck said. "If I'd stayed with the Giants, I wouldn't have gone to the Cubs. A lot of things happened in Chicago that were very special."

In fact, Beck's final save in 1998 came at the expense of San Francisco. Shooter got the last two outs in a tiebreaker game that won the wild card playoff berth for the Cubs.

After stints with the Red Sox and Padres, the pitcher retired in 2004 with 286 saves and a 3.30 ERA. Perhaps more than his numbers, his competitive spirit will be remembered. Fun loving and humorous off the field, Beck was a picture of intimidation on the mound. His unspoken message to his rivals was clear. "Nobody can beat me out there," the Giant once said. "And if you do, if you beat me once, you ain't going to beat me again. That's the attitude I take out there."

That approach made Beck effective even after his pitching arm showed its age, said Piazza, a longtime opponent who faced him many times. "He had a lot of confidence and a great disposition on the mound," the catcher said. "If you believe you're going to get someone out, that goes a long way."

After baseball, Shooter wore his scowling game face again as an actor in "Work Week," an independent film about gangsters and the mob.

But Beck's health plummeted in the three years following his retirement and the 38-year-old died at his Phoenix, Arizona home on June 23, 2007. His former wife Stacey Beck spoke of his cocaine addiction which he tried to overcome through interventions and rehabilitation.

"This disease stole from all of us the family man we loved," shared Stacey, who had two daughters with Rod. "It is our family's hope that our honesty about our personal tragedy can inspire others to get help; if not the addict, the spouses, parents and children who are so profoundly impacted."

Many from the Giants family attended Beck's funeral, honoring him not just as a baseball player but as a community-minded family man who devoted his time and money to helping children with AIDS.

"He'll always be remembered as one of the greatest Giants of all time," said Aurilia.

18

MARVIN BENARD

BENARD ROCKS THE YARD

POSITION: center field

SEASONS WITH GIANTS: 1995–2003

ACCOMPLISHMENTS: led Giants in runs (100), hits (163), stolen bases (27), and triples (5) in 1999

GAME OF HIS LIFE: July 2, 2000 versus Los Angeles Dodgers

A NEW ERA BEGAN for the orange and black in 2000 when the club moved into its new downtown home, though the team's early results at 24 Willie Mays Plaza were not what the Giants had in mind. Their much-anticipated opener fizzled when Los Angeles stole the park's first home run and win. San Francisco became the only big league team to lose its first six games at its own new yard. Not until 27 days later would the Giants win their first home contest. Even a presidential visit turned into a disappointment that month when a rainout postponed the game Bill Clinton came to see. Right fielder Ellis Burks wondered aloud if the team might have aroused supernatural ire by disturbing an ancient Indian burial ground.

"It was a tough way to start the year," said Marvin Benard, then playing in his sixth season with the team. "The Dodgers came in and beat us three times. We lost the next few and then one rained out. It seemed like we couldn't win a game at home to save our lives."

Like his team, Benard started the season in a disheartening funk. The slump was puzzling because the Nicaraguan-born center fielder played the best ball of his career in 1999. During the Giants' last year at Candlestick Park, Benard set career highs in hits, home runs, and stolen bases.

"I love Marvin to death. He busted his butt and played hard," said Giants broadcaster Ted Robinson. "He certainly wasn't as talented as Barry Bonds, Ellis Burks, or Stan Javier, but he played as hard as anybody and maximized his ability."

Early in the 2000 campaign, San Francisco signed the 29-year-old to an $11.1-million contract extension. But the ink wasn't yet dry on the three-year deal before the Giant seemed to hit the ballpark's new brick wall. His batting average, a healthy .290 in 1999, plummeted to .224 in April 2000. A missed sign here and a missed catch there hurt San Francisco in tight games the team lost. One errant throw even hit Benard in a sensitive spot below the belt. The blow struck hard enough to knock him to the ground in pain.

A year before, Benard was the greatest overachiever ever drafted in the 50th round. Then before he knew it, he had become a target for boo birds and angry callers on sports talk radio. Benard became so upset that he stopped talking to the media.

"It's hard not to take it personally," he said. "When they start booing you—especially when you've never been through it before—you don't know how to react or how to take it. You have no other way but to take it personally, because we're human. I wouldn't wish it on anyone. No one should ever get booed for trying their best."

A lack of effort after receiving his handsome contract was not the reason for his slump, Benard said. In fact, he believes the exact opposite may be true.

"I never understood until it happened to me," Benard said. "Guys sign these big contracts, and the next year they're stinking up the joint. People take it as, 'They got paid, now they don't care anymore,' but it's not that. It's because they're trying to do too much. Once you get a big contract, you say,

Marvin Benard's dramatic home run against the Dodgers in the game of his life put the 2000 Giants on course for a division championship. *Brace Photo*

'Oh man, I gotta do more,' and you end up pushing yourself too hard. You end up going backwards instead of forwards."

Benard's bat slowly heated up in the next two months. The center fielder lifted his average to a respectable .272. But San Francisco still languished in fourth place at the end of June. Then the leadoff hitter lifted his team and answered his critics with one dramatic swing against—who else?—Los Angeles. The Dodgers hit town to play their rivals in a three-game set. It was the first visit by Los Angeles since the boys in blue swept the Giants in their ballpark's debut homestand. The teams split the first two games before the July 2 series finale, a high-stakes contest for both clubs just one game apart in the standings.

Pitching for the Dodgers was the hard-throwing Eric Gagne, a future All-Star closer. In 2000, "The Beast" was a second-year starter in the Los Angeles rotation. Benard got San Francisco started with a single in the bottom of the first, hitting Gagne's high-90s heater sharply into left. He quickly stole second and then took third on an error by Dodgers catcher Todd Hundley. Bill Mueller brought him home with a sacrifice fly, and the Giants took an early 1-0 lead.

For San Francisco, Shawn Estes pitched five innings that were effective if not strong. The southpaw put 11 Dodgers on base, but gave up just one run. In the third, Estes dug himself into a giant hole, walking three batters in a row. He wiggled out of trouble by striking out Hundley and popping up shortstop Kevin Elster.

"I pitched about as bad as you could pitch with nobody on base and about as good as you could pitch with guys on base," said the pitcher. "I can't explain it."

Thanks to the Giants offense, Estes left the game leading, 4-1. On a day when Barry Bonds sat out, the team's second baseman fueled the action. Jeff Kent singled and scored in the fourth and homered over the center-field wall in the fifth. In the seventh, the future MVP drilled another shot into the left-field seats. But the Dodgers rallied twice against the San Francisco bullpen.

In the seventh, the visitors scored two against Giants lefty Aaron Fultz. In the next frame, Los Angeles struck again against pitcher Felix Rodriguez. Manager Dusty Baker was forced to summon Robb Nen with two runners on base. The sellout crowd groaned when the closer's wild pitch let the Dodgers tie the game, 5-5, though Nen retired five more batters to close out the Los Angeles eighth and ninth.

Hitless since the first, Benard led off in the bottom of the ninth. Baker had an attractive pinch hitter available in Bonds, but stuck with his leadoff man. The manager's loyalty to the center fielder through his slump riled impatient fans, but the biggest Benard bashers would get nothing to complain about this time.

Pitching for the Dodgers was Mike Fetters, a right-hander known for a curious ritual. Before every pitch, Fetters breathed heavily and whipped his head around sharply toward the batter. Opponents and spectators were surprised and amused by the routine, which the asthmatic pitcher used to control his breathing on the mound.

Benard worked the count to 2-2 and then connected on a forkball. The ball flew high and deep to right as he raced to first. Benard pumped his fist as the ball left the yard and 40,930 delighted fans erupted. A giant message screaming from the scoreboard said it all: "Marvin-ous!" A horde of joyful teammates met Benard at the plate and lifted him off his feet.

In the first great Dodgers bloodletting at 24 Willie Mays Plaza, San Francisco beat Los Angeles, 6-5.

"If I had to do it over again, I would throw the same pitch," said Fetters, who usually laid waste to left-handed batters. "It was a forkball a little down and I guess the guy was geared for it. It was a decent pitch, but he got me."

The home run was Benard's sixth of the year and only his third in the Giants' spacious new park.

"Marvin, the leadoff hitter, was the last guy you would think would hit one out to win it," said San Francisco shortstop Rich Aurilia. "He's a little guy, but not too little. That was a huge win for us."

The Game of My Life
By Marvin Benard

When it comes to highlights, that home run would be a favorite one because of the fact I grew up in Los Angeles as a Dodgers fan. So to be able to do something like that in the rivalry was something special.

Mike Fetters came in to pitch the ninth inning. He would take this big deep breath and his cheeks filled up with air. He looked like a blowfish. Then he'd snap his neck around. It was pretty interesting. We saw him do this and thought, "So, you want to show us up? Here we go!" Later we found out it was all a breathing exercise.

When I got to home plate, everybody jumped all over me and picked me up and smacked me on the head. That's when it really sunk in that something special had happened here. But it was bittersweet, because of the way I was struggling and getting booed. The last thing I wanted to do was celebrate with the fans. If I had it my way, I would have gone back into the dugout and high-fived my teammates. But they came to home plate and picked me up, so it was hard not to celebrate on the field.

I remember looking over at the Dodgers dugout. F.P. Santangelo was still in there with a little smile of his own. He grew up in Northern California as a Giants fan, and suddenly here he was playing against the Giants. I grew up a Dodgers fan and now I play for the Giants. He and I are friends and he was wearing a little smirk. I could tell that he was excited for me and that was pretty cool.

	1	2	3	4	5	6	7	8	9	R	H	E
Dodgers	0	0	0	1	0	0	2	2	0	5	13	1
Giants	1	0	0	2	1	0	1	0	1	6	10	1

Benard: 5 at-bats, 2 runs, 2 hits, 1 HR, 1 RBI

After Benard's walk-off homer, San Francisco got red hot. The team built an eight-game winning streak and won nine straight in late summer.

"Things starting turning around for us. It was an awesome feeling. Suddenly we came back and went on a huge roll," Benard said. "It seems like after that, we couldn't lose a game at home. We ended up having the best record in baseball at home, which was amazing after we started how we did."

Only one game over .500 before the July 2 contest, the Giants finished at 97-65, winning the National League West with the best record in baseball. San Francisco's final 11-game advantage over second-place Los Angeles was the biggest margin of victory the team had ever had.

The 2000 Giants set a franchise record with more than 3.31 million in attendance, nearly double their draw in the 1997 playoff run. In fact, the park that made splash hits and kayaks part of baseball sold out its entire inaugural season.

"It was a remarkable year," said Benard. "We had that theme song, 'Who Let the Dogs Out?' It got to the point where just to hear it was exciting, like the Robb Nen song ('Smoke on the Water'). It seemed like those two songs went hand in hand. We just kept winning and they kept playing those songs."

Benard credits his teammates for helping him shake off the jeers. "We all had confidence in Marvin," said Aurilia. "Any time you get a contract and you get some money and you don't perform up to par with what people expect or what they want, you're going to get criticism. Give Marvin credit for hanging in there and playing hard every time. He was a big part of us winning."

Benard's glorious game-winning homer notwithstanding, the hustling Giant never became the premier leadoff hitter the team had expected him to be. He finished the 2000 season batting .263, and averaged .259 for the next three years as injuries decreased his playing time.

"Marvin ended up getting a real bad rap in San Francisco," Robinson said. "Here's a guy drafted in the 50th round. He had no natural tools and was never a big prospect. Marvin forced his way through hard work and willpower to the big leagues."

Benard's big league career ended after 2003, though he played minor league ball in 2004 with the Toronto Blue Jays organization. That same year, his name first surfaced in published reports about the Bay Area Laboratory Co-Operative. The Mitchell Report, baseball's most comprehensive accounting of the game's steroids era, also alleged Benard's use of performance-enhancing drugs.

Benard eventually admitted using steroids in 2002 while recovering from knee surgery, a decision he calls "stupid" and "embarrassing."

"If you look at every decade, there's some sort of a scandal that happens, all the way back to 1919," he said. "I think time takes care of everything. It's going to come to a conclusion and whatever that is, hopefully people will let bygones be bygones."

Benard retired to Washington state, where he had settled with his wife and children during his Giants days. Someday he might like to get back into the big leagues, which he enjoyed despite the adversity.

"I was the kind of guy who was supposed to play half a season and get released and find something else to do," he said. "I'm proud of the fact that I worked my butt off to get where I got, and I'm thankful to a lot of people who believed in me."

19

ROBB NEN

"BASEBALL WARRIOR"

POSITION: pitcher

SEASONS WITH GIANTS: 1998–2002

ACCOMPLISHMENTS: All-Star in 1998, 1999, and 2002; led National League in saves (45) in 2001; set Giants career record with 206 saves

GAME OF HIS LIFE: October 7, 2002 versus Atlanta Braves

ON A STEAMY NIGHT in Atlanta, a two-run edge never looked so small. San Francisco led the Braves, 3-1, in a do-or-die playoff game on October 7, 2002. Closer Robb Nen took the mound in the ninth as the Giants tried to finish off their foes, but the inning did not start well for the pitching star.

Nen fired heater after heater to Rafael Furcal in a seven-pitch battle. Atlanta's leadoff hitter finally knocked a chopper up the middle, fielded by Jeff Kent, but the second baseman's throw to first flew off target. The Braves shortstop reached first on the error.

While Atlanta's tomahawk chop riff blasted throughout Turner Field, 45,203 Braves fans waved their arms and tomahawks to the mindless beat. Then the speedy Furcal stole second, and Atlanta's Julio Franco cracked a single to right, advancing Furcal to third. With no outs, the Braves had the tying runs on base, with the meat of their order coming up.

The Giants and their most ardent fans could be forgiven a foreboding sense of doom, because the 32-year-old Nen and his teammates had been in this exact situation seven weeks before, and that game's ending tormented them. In that contest, San Francisco had also led in the ninth, 3-1, before Atlanta's Chipper Jones delivered a two-out, two-run single to tie it up. A lengthy storm struck in the tenth and eventually rained out the game. Deprived of the win, the Giants were delayed in Atlanta well past midnight and later forced to wearily board a flight to Florida that arrived after sunrise.

On deck for the Braves in the playoff game was none other than the same Chipper Jones, batting a gaudy .500 against Nen with a home run in 12 lifetime at-bats. The season hung in the balance. Nen's response to this crisis showed the unflappable attitude that sets top-flight closers apart from, well, normal human beings who react typically to stress and pressure.

"You can't worry about what happens," he said simply. "It was part of my job. There are runners on, now I have to get the next out." After all, the keys to closing games, Nen said, are "a short memory and confidence in your stuff."

Those qualities helped Nen save 314 games in his ten-year career, 206 of them in his five years with San Francisco, a Giants record. General manager Brian Sabean acquired the right-hander from the salary-dumping Florida Marlins after the 1997 season for three minor leaguers. Perhaps the best trade of Sabean's career, the deal was San Francisco's equivalent of the Ocean's Eleven casino heist.

Nen's fastball reached 98 mph, but it was his slider that made him unique. Most pitchers throw their breaking balls in the 70s and 80s. Nen's slider shot by in the low 90s, and looked exactly like his fastball until it plunged toward the dirt. Then there was his delivery, which featured an unusual slide step, instead of a kick, and an odd toe tap. Together the combination baffled his opponents' timing.

A three-time All-Star, Nen led the National League with 45 saves in 2001. When he was in top form, there was no better closer in baseball.

"That guy Nen, I hate to even see him warming up," said Felipe Alou when he managed the Montreal Expos. "He's the guy you least want to see

Robb Nen's clutch performance helped the Giants advance in the 2002 playoffs.
Jamie Squire/Getty Images

out there. There are guys out there who are going to get you saves. But the stuff this guy has is wicked. It isn't hittable."

All the while the pitcher kept a cool-as-ice demeanor on the mound, never showing up opponents with theatrics and rarely showing any emotion at all.

"Robb Nen is one of the few (closers) I've seen that isn't a little on the crazy side," said Dusty Baker, the Giants manager during Nen's San Francisco years. "I'm sure he has some crazy on the inside, but he doesn't show it on the outside."

Nen was part of a core of stars who raised high expectations for the 2002 club. After near misses in 1998 and 2001 and quick playoff losses in 1997 and 2000, the team's brass set the bar high. "It's time to get off our asses," Sabean announced. Owner Peter Magowan publicly stated he expected the club to win at least the National League pennant. Such comments irked Baker even though they proved prophetic.

After a slow start, the Giants got hot in the second half, winning 18 of their last 25 and their first-ever wild card playoff berth. Nen, true to form, saved 43 games and won six more. The team finished the season with eight straight wins, roaring into a fierce National League Division Series against the Braves.

San Francisco won the opener in Atlanta, 8-5. The Braves took the next two, pushing the Giants to the brink of elimination in the five-game set. Then San Francisco prevailed, 8-3, in the must-win Game 4 at 24 Willie Mays Plaza. The series returned to Atlanta for the fifth and decisive game. Starting for the Braves was Kevin Millwood, an 18-game winner in 2002 with a mid-90s fastball, a hard slider, and a change-up. The All-Star quickly dispatched San Francisco in the first, retiring the side in order on two fly balls and a strikeout. The Giants gave the ball to Russ Ortiz, their most reliable starter in 2002, who opened the game in his typical fashion: throwing hard, walking enough batters to make his manager nervous, striking out even more, and somehow escaping with minimal damage. Ortiz walked sluggers Gary Sheffield and Chipper Jones in the first, but popped up Andruw Jones to retire the side, and the duel for the National League Championship Series was on.

Bonds fired up the Giants offense in the second with a single to left, and later scored on a two-out hit by Reggie Sanders. Two innings later, Bonds crushed a Millwood fastball for his third home run of the series, and the Giants led, 2-0. Meanwhile, Ortiz shut down Atlanta through the fifth frame, retiring eight straight Braves at one point and striking out five. Baker pulled his starter after Andruw Jones and Vinny Castilla singled in the sixth. San Francisco's Aaron Fultz allowed a RBI single to Mark DeRosa, which cut the Giants' lead to 2-1.

J.T. Snow doubled in the seventh, later to score on Kenny Lofton's sacrifice fly. San Francisco led, 3-1. But the bullpens kept a lid on the game as it approached the late innings. In the ninth, the Giants gave the ball to their closer with a two-run lead.

Kent actually made a fine play in the ninth to get to Furcal's grounder, and while his throw to first was poor, the replay reveals that Snow stayed on the bag just long enough to catch it. The play was extremely close, but the umpire should have called Furcal out.

"That's part of the game," Nen said. "Kent makes a great play, maybe the umpire misses it, but I could have walked him just as easily."

After Franco singled, Sheffield came to bat representing the winning run. The match-up pitted power against power. Sheffield took a murderous cut at the first pitch, a hanging slider, and came up empty. Nen then planted a blazing fastball low on the outside corner of the zone, called strike two, a perfect pitch. The batter fouled off the next one, and then Nen fired a high heater near Sheffield's hands. The Brave swung right through it, and the closer had his first out.

"That was a key part of the inning," Nen said. "Gary was one of the premier players in the game, so it definitely sticks in my head. I knew I didn't want to give in to him and give him something good to hit. To be aggressive with Gary was my key focus in that situation."

As the switch-hitting Chipper Jones came to bat once more, Nen admits he flashed back to his August disappointment.

"I remembered how Chipper beat me two months before," Nen said. "I knew it was the same situation, so I was a little more emotional than usual, knowing what was at stake. It was fun."

Nen's all-business, "what, me worry?" attitude faced an exceptionally challenging test. The base runners, the Giant-killing Jones at bat, potential playoff elimination, Magowan's demand for the pennant, and Atlanta's incessant tomahawk chop song—it's a wonder the damned recording didn't wear out—all combined to heat the pressure past the boiling point.

On Baker's orders, Snow played on the line at first. From there he was more likely to prevent a game-tying extra-base hit into the corner, though less likely to stop a single through the hole that would put the winning run on base. Either decision could be right or wrong. San Francisco would find out soon enough.

Nen threw a fastball past Jones on the corner, called strike one. Then a play occurred so quickly that most of the Giants didn't see what happened. On the next pitch, Jones scorched the ball down the first-base line Snow picked it clean, raised the ball in his throwing hand, and chased the base runner Franco halfway to second before firing to Rich Aurilia. The shortstop tagged Franco out, and Snow leaped high into the air with his arms raised. Suddenly Nen and the Giants realized that Snow had managed to touch first base, retiring Jones, before he threw the ball. Their Gold Gloved first baseman had turned a scintillating double play, and the ballgame was over.

For the first time in 13 years, San Francisco had won a playoff series, and the team joined Snow in a joyful celebration.

The Game of My Life
By Robb Nen

For me they were all a blast, but any time you played the Atlanta Braves, it was going to be tough, especially with me. I got myself in trouble and I had to battle out of it. Those were great games, and some fun things to think back on and remember.

Everybody was pumped up for that game. I always put a lot of pressure on myself. The pressure was what made my job fun for me. It wasn't fun when I blew a save or something like that, but it kept the excitement high knowing how much every game was going to mean.

I think Sheffield's little bat waggle and my toe tap screwed him up a little bit timing wise. Two wrongs made it right for me there.

Every time I pitched to Chipper, he hit me real well. He beat me up all the time, so I tried to do some different things. I wanted to throw a slider in on his hands to jam him or get him to swing through it.

He hit the ball to J.T. and the funny thing is a lot of guys on the field didn't realize J.T. touched first base before he threw to second. I was running to first and saw him jump up and said, "Hey, what's going on here?"

The guys all knew what I went through before. After the game, a lot of them came up to me and said, "Nice job—we knew you could do it." There were hugs and champagne and beer flying all over the place. It was a chance to really have some fun with the guys. That meant a lot to me.

Those are always the best times, the celebrations in the clubhouse afterwards, pouring champagne, drinking, and having a good time with your teammates. You work all season to get that. I cherished every one of those.

	1	2	3	4	5	6	7	8	9	R	H	E
Giants	0	1	0	1	0	0	1	0	0	3	6	2
Braves	0	0	0	0	0	1	0	0	0	1	7	0

Nen: save, 1 inning pitched, 1 hit, 0 runs, 0 walks, 1 strikeout

---

For the Giants, the win was a milestone in many respects. After ten years together, Magowan's ownership group and Baker celebrated their first playoff series victory, as did Bonds and many other players. San Francisco earned a measure of revenge against Atlanta, which had plagued the Giants ever since winning the ferocious National League West division race of 1993. And the win set the club on course for the National League pennant and a thrilling World Series appearance.

Only later did the public learn the playoffs' added significance for Nen, who was pitching despite a labrum tear in his throwing shoulder. Nen's continued play led to serious rotator cuff damage. The Giants kept the injury secret until the off-season in an attempt to prevent their opponents from taking advantage of the injury.

"He didn't tell us that much, either," said Baker. "We knew he was having a little shoulder problem, but we had no clue it was that fierce. He refused to tell me or anybody."

At first the problem caused Nen pain and required a longer warm-up. Later it began to affect his velocity. Despite the injury, Nen saved three of the Giants' victories against the Cardinals in the National League Championship Series, and closed out two San Francisco wins in the World Series.

"I figured you get to this step once or twice in your whole career," Nen said. "I wasn't going to back out of it. I was going to keep throwing and getting people out and worry about the consequences later."

The save he attempted in Game 6 of the World Series was as close to mission impossible as they come, even for a healthy pitcher. The Giants gave Nen the ball with a one-run lead, but the Anaheim Angels had the tying run on third and the go-ahead run on second with nobody out in the eighth. On top of that, the closer's arm just wasn't the same.

"By the time we got to the World Series, his fastball was down to 89 or 90 mph," said Giants broadcaster Jon Miller. "He was doing it with blood, sweat, and tears."

Nen underwent surgery in the off-season and hoped to return for spring training. The shoulder wouldn't permit it. More surgeries, rehab, and physical therapy filled the next two years.

"From the World Series on, it was tough," Nen said. "There were three surgeries and lots of rehab in that time. There were a lot of disappointments. I tried to battle back as much as I could, but it just didn't quite work out. It was frustrating to sit around, watch my teammates play, and not be able to help the team win."

The Giants released Nen after his contract expired in 2004. Shortly after, he announced his retirement at age 35.

"Robb Nen sacrificed his arm to help the Giants get to the World Series in 2002. There's just no other way to look at it," said Miller. "He was a great baseball warrior, that's for sure."

San Francisco honored the pitcher with a "Robb Nen Day" farewell in 2005, and placed a plaque commemorating his 300th save on the McCovey Cove boardwalk in 2006. As a tribute to one of his favorite-ever Giants, clubhouse manager Mike Murphy hung Nen's jersey in the team's locker room for years, whether he was with the team or not.

"Without a doubt, my biggest high in this job was watching Robbie do what he did that fall, and without a doubt, my biggest low is knowing he can't ever do anything like it again," said pitching coach Dave Righetti.

"You want to believe, if it were you, you'd do the same," said teammate Kirk Rueter. "But I don't think any of us knows. All we know is that he did it, and we know we just respect him so much for it."

So do the fans. Each time Nen returns to 24 Willie Mays Plaza, the crowd greets him with warmth and enthusiasm.

"Those fans are the greatest fans in baseball for me, the way they treated me and my family," Nen said. "They know their game. Whenever I go in that place, so many people recognize me and say, 'Hey Robb, we appreciate what you did, you had a great career.' That makes me feel good."

Nen would do it all again, he said on numerous occasions.

"It didn't work out the way I wanted, with us failing to win the World Series, but I wouldn't change what I did. My career lasted a long time, I did all right, and I was able to enjoy it," he said.

20

KENNY LOFTON

"LET A SLEEPING DOG LIE"

POSITION: center field

SEASONS WITH GIANTS: 2002

ACCOMPLISHMENTS: six-time All-Star; scored tying run and delivered game-winning RBI in decisive game of 2002 National League Championship Series

GAME OF HIS LIFE: October 14, 2002 versus St. Louis Cardinals

---

AN EXCITED AND NOISY crowd waved a sea of rally towels even before the game got underway, and thousands of ticketless fans tried to squeeze into the free viewing area behind the right-field fence. A fleet of canoes and kayaks jostled for position in McCovey Cove. The ballpark quietly imported cases of champagne, storing them under lock and key.

Giants fever was running wild at 24 Willie Mays Plaza, and for good reason. San Francisco had swept the first two games of the 2002 National League Championship Series in St. Louis, utterly silencing legions of red-clad Cardinals fans at their own yard.

Barry Bonds struck such fear into the hearts of St. Louis pitching that southpaw Steve Kline expressed his yearning for invisible baseballs to throw past the slugger. The desperate Cardinals walked the left fielder three times during the third contest in San Francisco, which St. Louis won. But the strategy backfired on the Cardinals in Game 4. After manager Tony La Russa ordered a free pass to Bonds with two outs in the eighth, catcher Benito Santiago delivered the hit of his life, a monstrous two-run homer that put the Giants ahead for good.

"It's a dream coming true. It's just unbelievable," Santiago said. "I feel like I'm 13 years old, jumping all over the place."

He may have felt like a kid, but Santiago and his teammates swung their bats like men, making St. Louis pay dearly for walking Bonds ten times in the series. Shortstop Rich Aurilia hit .333 in the NLCS and third baseman David Bell hit a mammoth .412. Meanwhile, Giants pitchers held a powerful Cardinals lineup to a manageable .257 batting average.

Leading three games to one, San Francisco appeared to be hitting on all cylinders, needing one more win to complete its drive for the National League pennant. One Giant, though, wasn't enjoying the ride as much as the others. Leadoff hitter Kenny Lofton was mired in an 0-for-16 slump, batting a measly .118 for the first four games. The center fielder had hit well enough in the opener, with a single and a homer against pitcher Matt Morris. But he infuriated the St. Louis dugout by pausing to admire his shot sailing over the fence.

To an old-school skipper like La Russa, that's felony contempt, and the Cardinals let the Giants know it. When Lofton came to bat again in the fifth, St. Louis pitcher Mike Crudale threw him a fastball high and tight. Lofton exchanged angry words with the hurler and catcher Mike Matheny. The argument drew players from both teams onto the field, bringing the game to a screeching halt.

"We don't start nothing, but we don't take nothing," declared Giants manager Dusty Baker. Though to hear the Cardinals tell it, Lofton "pimped" his home run and overreacted to the inside pitch. St. Louis pitching coach Dave Duncan branded Lofton "a classless act in more ways than one." La Russa suggested that Lofton should pay the $500 fines the league levied upon the managers for the shouting match. "Both teams know it was instigated by a player who was being foolish," he said.

An ecstatic Kenny Lofton celebrates his pennant-clinching hit against St. Louis in 2002. *Jeff Haynes/AP/Getty Images*

"That's bogus for someone to even say that," Lofton retorted. "Did I throw the pitch? I hit a home run. Next time I come to the plate, the first pitch is up and in. Now who's classless?"

"They threw it, I didn't," he continued. "I ain't the pitcher, so how did I instigate it?" The center fielder concluded with a message for the opposition: "I ain't no punk. Tell 'em that."

Many observers noted La Russa's prowess in mind games, speculating that he crafted his comments to wreak havoc on Lofton's psyche. If so, perhaps it worked, for his bat seemed to freeze immediately. The strategy did not surprise the veteran.

"We were kicking their butts at the time and they had to do something to try to upset me or piss me off," Lofton said. "That's what they did." For the next three and a half games, the Giant failed to get a hit, striking out four times.

Game 5 would be different as Lofton broke out of his slump. In a thrilling one-run contest on October 14, Lofton sparked the San Francisco offense. Starting for the Cardinals again, Morris retired Lofton in the first. The All-Star threw three perfect frames to start the contest, while San Francisco's Kirk Rueter surrendered five hits but no runs. Then Lofton led off the fourth, and to the Giants' shock and amazement, Morris beaned him with his first pitch, a 93-mph heater. Lofton reacted calmly, but the Giants believed that Morris targeted the 35-year-old. The hurler still maintains he did not, though he admits that his anger affected his pitch and says he's come to a new perspective on his old foe.

"Kenny didn't look at the ball (in Game 1) any longer than he has in previous years or previous homers," Morris said. "It's just his style of play. The more I watch, the more I see how consistent he is. That's his approach. He's an unbelievable player.

"I think it really got to me," Morris said. "Getting mad at him got me out of my game plan. That was probably his whole strategy, and it worked. I let my thought process get too personal between him and me, rather than concentrating on executing pitches. When I hit him, it wasn't as intentional as it looked."

Lofton didn't score in the inning, though the incident marked a critical turn in the game. He delivered nothing but hits the rest of the way, and two of the blows would torture his rivals.

Santiago walked to lead off the fifth, and two outs later, Bell doubled to the right field corner. Santiago raced towards third as fast as his 37-year-old legs would carry him, intending to dash home, yet he never got the chance. Cardinals third baseman Miguel Cairo, without the ball, collided with him as he rounded the bag, causing the catcher to stumble and scamper back to third. Santiago raised his arms in protest and umpire Jeff Nelson called obstruction on the play, yet he ruled that the runner would not have scored without the collision. He awarded the catcher, but only third base. Santiago and the Giants howled, though the decision stood. When Rueter grounded out to end the inning, the game remained a scoreless tie, and fans filled the park with angry boos.

"In a moment like that, you have two choices," Bell said. "You can get frustrated and upset, or keep playing the game and figure out a way to win. In this game, you really have to have a short memory. I think that was a credit to our team that we didn't let something like that slow us down."

Both teams dodged trouble in the sixth. In the top half, the Cardinals put two runners aboard on a walk and a hit. But Rueter, a master of escape, wiggled out of the jam by inducing a grounder from left fielder Eli Marrero. Rueter pumped his arms and roared with the crowd as he walked off the field. His night was over after six shutout frames.

Lofton singled in the home half, his first hit since his Game 1 homer. Then Morris hit Aurilia on his left hand with a 90-mph fastball. With nobody out and runners on first and second, San Francisco looked for a productive inning. However, second baseman Jeff Kent grounded into a double play, and after another walk to Bonds, Santiago grounded out to end the frame.

At last, St. Louis struck for a run in the seventh against new Giants pitcher Felix Rodriguez. Matheny doubled against the flamethrower and later scored on a sacrifice fly. With the game's first run, the Cardinals took a rare lead, and the bad break that prevented Santiago from scoring earlier now loomed large.

Yet San Francisco would overcome the controversial call with Lofton-fueled rallies in the final innings. The center fielder batted again with one out in the Giants' eighth. Morris threw two beautiful curveballs to jump ahead, 0-2. Then the pitcher grooved a 95-mph fastball right down the pipe. Lofton whacked it into center field and San Francisco had itself a rally.

"I was thinking about throwing another curve, then I tried to get a fastball off the plate," Morris said. Things would get worse for the pitcher in the frame, though he said his fat pitch to Lofton was the one he regretted most.

After Aurilia singled to left, Morris hit a batter for the third time in the game. His 76-mph curveball hit Kent in the back, and even the Giants didn't accuse the pitcher of throwing at him this time, because the mistake loaded the bases for their most lethal weapon. Pitching to Bonds with the World Series on the line was the last thing La Russa wanted to do, but the Cardinals' dreadful situation left him no choice. St. Louis had a one-run lead and nowhere to put the slugger. Morris threw a 95-mph heater away, and Bonds clubbed it 380 feet to the warning track in left. In many parks, it would have been a grand slam, though at 24 Willie Mays Plaza, the drive became a sacrifice fly. Lofton easily scored and returned to a barrage of high-fives in a joyful dugout. The Giants were on the board; heading to the ninth, the ballgame was tied, 1-1.

San Francisco's Tim Worrell made short work of the Cardinals in the top of the inning. In their typical stress-inducing fashion, the Giants waited until two were out in the bottom half to start their pennant-clinching rally. Still in the game and throwing hard, Morris fired a 93-mph heater to Bell, who ripped a line drive to left for a single. Next up was right fielder Shawon

Dunston, an 18-season veteran who had never reached a World Series. In a carbon copy of the previous at-bat, Morris threw the same fastball and Dunston hit the same line drive for another single.

That advanced the winning run to second and brought up the man the Cardinals loved to hate. On top of the Giants dugout steps, Baker got an in-game analysis from his three-year-old son, Darren. "Daddy, one more hit from Kenny Lofton and we win the game," the young Giants batboy told his father. La Russa realized that, too, and finally took the ball from Morris. The skipper summoned Kline from the bullpen in hopes of reaching a tenth inning.

Lofton looked for a slider from the St. Louis southpaw, which Kline delivered on his very first pitch. Lofton pounced on the 82-mph offering, muscling a one-hopper into right field. In a moment San Francisco fans will remember forever, right fielder J.D. Drew grabbed the ball and fired while Bell furiously charged around third. "You got to score, David, you got to score!" Lofton screamed across the diamond at his teammate. Bell dove head first into home plate, and the throw arrived off-line. The third baseman scored the winning run. Bell bounced to his feet and embraced Aurilia as their teammates burst onto the field. A deafening ovation threatened to topple the ballpark. The Giants had won the pennant.

"I'll never forget that as long as I live," said Bell. "Running from second to home, not knowing if it would be a close play or not, diving across the plate, and finally the relief and excitement of going to the World Series, it was the best feeling I've ever had in the game. Nothing else even compares to it.

"I really thought it would be a close play," he said. "Not until my hand touched the plate did I know that it was really going to happen. The fans were incredible throughout the whole postseason. That made it extra special, to do it in front of them."

Lofton pumped his arms and jumped about wildly before he even reached first base. For a moment, he stared down the defeated Cardinals in their dugout in what his opponents perceived as an unspoken taunt. Then his teammates swept him up like a tidal wave, lifting him off his feet in pure ecstasy.

"He had a roller coaster series but in the end he got the big hit," said San Francisco general manager Brian Sabean. "It's poetic justice that he got the hit after being drilled. Why they chose that point to drill him is amazing to me. It came back to haunt them."

Fans around the park waved signs with slogans such as "Bye Bye Birdies" and "Kenny was right!" In the St. Louis clubhouse, the Cardinals admitted that Lofton's highlight-reel hit was salt in their wounds. "He's the only guy I didn't want to beat me," Kline said. "I don't like that guy."

Lofton tried to downplay the ill will in his postgame comments. "It's over, we're going to the World Series, and all that other stuff don't matter," he said.

Though he couldn't resist one parting shot at his foes: "Somebody said, 'Let a sleeping dog lie.'"

The Game of My Life
By Kenny Lofton

St. Louis was frustrated and they thought someone was showing them up. That wasn't the case, but that's the way the game goes. When their players do it, it's okay. But when the other team does it, they get upset. It's just baseball. I don't want to make a big deal out of it just because that's what somebody else wants me to do.

I'd seen Kline before so I had a pretty good idea what he was going to try to do. The last time I faced Kline, he threw me a couple of sliders and I swung at and missed some bad pitches. He was going to throw the fastball and throw a nice little slider. I told myself, if he throws a nice little slider over the plate, I'm going to swing at it.

There wasn't really a whole lot going through my mind. I was just telling myself, "See the ball, hit the ball." Whatever pitch I saw, as long as it was a strike, I was going to go ahead and take a good swing at it. I put the ball in play and that was all it took.

It was pretty exciting because the team was going to the World Series, and a lot of our guys hadn't been there before at that point. Being in the World Series with a team you feel good about is very special. The guys that I played with were awesome. They all had the attitude that you look for in a winning team. Everyone was really gung ho about trying to get that ring. That's what it's all about.

	1	2	3	4	5	6	7	8	9	R	H	E
Cardinals	0	0	0	0	0	0	1	0	0	1	9	0
Giants	0	0	0	0	0	0	0	1	1	2	7	0

Lofton: 4 at-bats, 1 run, 3 hits, 1 RBI

After the game ended, the visiting players lingered sadly in their dugout, watching the euphoric Giants dance about on the field. Though the Cardinals won 97 games and reached the National League Championship Series, the 2002 season and its ending were bitter for them.

"We failed in the postseason," La Russa said. "They outplayed us in every category."

Yet there was far more pain than that for St. Louis. Two members of the Cardinals organization died during the '02 campaign. Veteran broadcaster Jack Buck, 77, succumbed to a variety of health problems in June, a loss that deeply saddened the St. Louis community. Shocking, though, was the sudden passing of 33-year-old pitcher Darryl Kile, who died four days later in his Chicago hotel room of an undetected coronary blockage.

Especially hurt by the loss was Morris, a close friend of Kile and his teammate for three years. The pitcher honored his late comrade by wearing his initials and his number 57 on his hat. Kannon Kile, Darryl's five-year-old son, attended the playoffs in a pint-sized St. Louis jersey, providing the Cardinals an emotional lift. "Don't give up," the batboy told the players after St. Louis lost the first two games of the NLCS.

Despite handcuffing the Giants for most of the night, Morris was the losing pitcher in the finale. Sullenly, he sat on the dugout bench watching the celebration.

"Spending the off-season thinking about it wasn't fun," Morris said. "I was able to look myself in the mirror and be proud of what I did, but I'm there to win the game."

While the Giants won the series by four games to one, they didn't consider the hard-fought victory a blowout. "Not at all," said first baseman J.T. Snow. "What a team they had. We had to work for it. They didn't give us anything. They should be glad with the year they had. They went through some tough times."

San Francisco appeared headed for tough times in 2002 before acquiring Lofton from the Chicago White Sox on July 28. In exchange for two minor leaguers, the Giants got a six-time All-Star for the rest of the year.

Before the deadline-beating deal, third-place San Francisco was six games out of first. With Lofton in a Giants uniform for the next two months, the team kicked into high gear, finishing the regular season with a big winning streak and a wild-card playoff berth. The center fielder drilled a home run in his first Giants at-bat, and seemed to bring San Francisco the catalyst atop the batting order that the club had lacked.

"I brought what I do," Lofton said. "I go out there and try to get on base any way I can and try to help spark the team."

A longtime Cleveland Indian, Lofton also played in the 1995 World Series and has reached the playoffs 11 times in his 17-year career.

"There's no question what Kenny Lofton does. What he did in Cleveland all those years, he came over here and did the same thing," said Bonds. "The guy's always been a threat because he can go deep, he can bunt, he can still run, he can steal bases for you. That's what you need. Without a leadoff hitter, it's tough to win games. He's been able to win everywhere he's gone."

As a Giant, Lofton played just 63 games. San Francisco barely got to know the reclusive star. Born to a 14-year-old mother, Lofton was raised by his grandmother. They lived in the projects of East Chicago on the widow's Social Security money. After the 2002 season, the Giants moved in another direction. San Francisco signed the younger Ray Durham as a leadoff hitter and the harder-hitting Marquis Grissom to play center field.

Lofton bounced between seven teams in the next five years, reaching the postseason four more times before retiring in 2007.

21

RICH AURILIA

WITH HIS LUMBER AND HIS LEATHER

POSITION: shortstop, third base

SEASONS WITH GIANTS: 1995–2003, 2007–2009

ACCOMPLISHMENTS: All-Star in 2001; won Silver Slugger award in 2001; led National League in hits (206) in 2001; led National League shortstops in putouts (246) in 2001, led National League shortstops in fielding percentage (.980) in 2002

GAME OF HIS LIFE: October 23, 2002 versus Anaheim Angels

SAN FRANCISCO'S 2002 POSTSEASON was a thrilling and chilling ride, full of close, exciting games that racked the nerves of players and fans. From Robb Nen's heart-stopping Atlanta save to Kenny Lofton's pennant-clinching hit, the Giants seemed to claw for everything they got.

"This is the only way we can win," said Giants general manager Brian Sabean during the championship celebration. The final National League Championship Series game against the Cardinals was the team's third straight one-run contest. More suspenseful action followed in the World Series against the Angels, and San Francisco and Anaheim split two one-run games at Edison Field—to open the series. But when the Fall Classic shifted to San Francisco, the Angels erupted in a 10-4 blowout. Another loss would all but doom the Giants in the series. Despite pageantry, fanfare and a ThunderStix noisemaker giveaway, great anxiety filled 24 Willie Mays Plaza on October 23 before a critical fourth game.

"Livan Hernandez got hit pretty hard in Game 3, but we knew in Game 4 we had Kirk Rueter, one of the most competitive guys I've ever met," said Rich Aurilia. "He knew how to win and how to get people out. We were confident having him go to the mound."

Rueter's outing would be essential in a game San Francisco badly needed. Many Giants players contributed in another gripping, one-run thriller. Though all night long, the team's 31-year-old shortstop was in the middle of the action. Without Aurilia's lumber and leather, the contest would have ended very differently.

A hit and an error gave Anaheim an early chance in the first, though "Woody" retired the side by inducing the dangerous Troy Glaus to ground out.

"I just tried to go into it with the same attitude I had for all the regular season and my other postseason starts," said Rueter. "I try and keep the ball down, let my defense work, give the guys a chance to win, and keep it close."

In the bottom of the first, San Francisco threatened, too. Lofton and Aurilia singled against Angels pitcher John Lackey. The Giants had little history against the rookie starting on his 24th birthday, although he had pitched two innings in relief in the wild second game in Anaheim. Lackey's strategy against San Francisco was a popular one: walk Barry Bonds and make someone else beat him. The pitcher did just that in his early jam, and it worked because Benito Santiago grounded into a rally-killing double play.

The Angels tagged Rueter for a run in the second, hitting three straight singles followed by David Eckstein's sacrifice fly. An inning later with a runner on, Glaus drilled a 2-0 fastball deep to center. The ball sailed over a leaping Lofton into the first row of the bleachers, straight into the glove of a most unhappy Giants fan. San Francisco's home crowd quietly cringed and writhed. Anaheim leading, 3-0, was not what most patrons paid to see.

The home team rallied again in the bottom of the third. After Lofton singled, Aurilia smacked a double into left field. Once again, the Angels

Rich Aurilia contributed three hits and helped turn three double plays in the Giants' win over the Angels in Game 4 of the 2002 World Series. *Brace Photo*

chose to load the bases by walking Bonds, and once again, Santiago hit into a twin killing to end the threat. The furious Giants catcher smashed his helmet in frustration.

"When I hit into that second double play, I didn't want to go back to the dugout," Santiago said. "I wanted to jump up there and be with the fans. But you can't put your head down. I went back to the dugout and thought, 'Don't think about it. You might get a chance to win the game.'"

A chance for redemption would arrive sooner than Santiago knew, but first San Francisco had to quiet the Angels' noisy bats. Woody got it started by throwing a perfect fourth, and got a lift from Aurilia to help him through the fifth. After Anaheim's Garret Anderson beat out a ground ball to third, the slugger Glaus came up for another duel with Rueter. This time the Angels third baseman scorched a grounder which the shortstop snared. Aurilia and his mates turned two, and the tide began to turn.

Fortune favored the Giants in the bottom of the fifth. Rueter led off with a swinging bunt that bounced off the plate and spun away from both Lackey and catcher Bengie Molina. The ball didn't travel 20 feet but put Woody on first. Lofton followed with a bunt right up the third base line, which rolled and rolled and died near third, fair by just a whisker. That brought up Aurilia, two for two, to face Lackey again. The Giant cracked his third straight hit, a liner to right-center field. Rueter raced home while Lofton took third, bringing up Jeff Kent. San Francisco's second baseman drove home another run with a sacrifice to right.

By this time, Anaheim's incessant walks to Bonds surprised no one, though the crowd waved rubber chickens and loudly booed the move. The table was set for Santiago again, and the catcher finally feasted. Santiago ripped a single to center that sent Aurilia racing home. The sliding shortstop beat the throw as the Giants tied the game.

"Benito had been doing the job for us all postseason hitting behind Barry," Aurilia said. "We were just glad he was one for three in that situation because the one was a big one to tie the ballgame."

Rueter lasted one more inning, which started with Scott Spiezio's single to center. Woody rebounded by striking out second baseman Benji Gil. Next was Molina, who had singled against Rueter in the second. Aurilia conferenced with his pitcher before the catcher's next at-bat.

"I'd just been watching Molina and what he was trying to do," the All-Star shortstop said. "I told Kirk, 'This guy tries to shoot the ball to right field with guys on first. If he hits it there, make sure you get to first so we can turn a double play.'"

A few pitches later, the Giants got their wish. Molina hit a screamer to the best hands on their team. First baseman J.T. Snow, playing shallow, stopped the ball and threw to second. Aurilia fired back to Rueter who beat the runner to first base. San Francisco's double play was among the slickest in the series. A full house screamed approval as a beaming Woody pumped his fist.

"When I got that double play, the emotions just came out," said a still-smiling Rueter after the game.

Aurilia nearly put the Giants ahead when he batted in the sixth. Batting for Rueter, Tom Goodwin walked, stole second and took third on a deep fly ball. Then the shortstop hit a broken-bat liner which Glaus barely reached. The towering third baseman needed all his height to rob Aurilia of extra bases.

"The way Woody was pitching, I was just upset that ball didn't get over Glaus' head," Aurilia said. "If he wasn't 6-foot-8, or whatever he is, we could have gotten Woody the win."

San Francisco's bullpen kept it quiet in the Angels' seventh and eighth. Felix Rodriguez and Tim Worrell pitched a perfect inning each. Anaheim turned to its rookie sensation Francisco Rodriguez, the 20-year-old who debuted just three weeks earlier. The hard-throwing righty had never won a regular-season game, but already had five wins in the 2002 postseason. The Giants hadn't managed a single hit against "K-Rod" yet. In the seventh, he mowed down Kent, Bonds, and Santiago in order.

But when the Angels sent him back for the eighth, Snow dug out a slider for a single to right field. A passed ball put Snow on second for David Bell. The third baseman delivered a clutch single up the middle. Snow sprinted home, beating a good throw from center fielder Darin Erstad. San Francisco swung ahead, 4-3, for the first time that night. Only three outs stood between the Giants and the win. Manager Dusty Baker summoned his closer, Nen. Deep Purple's "Smoke on the Water" blasted as he jogged out to the mound.

Nen got Spiezio to pop out to third, but the Angels would not go quietly. Pinch hitter Adam Kennedy singled to put the tying run on base. When Brad Fullmer tried to bring him in, he knocked a check-swing grounder straight to short. Aurilia took it to second himself before firing to Snow again. Ironically, the shortstop's easiest double play ended the hard-fought game. The smiling Giants exchanged high-fives on the grass. Excited yet exhausted, 42,703 fans gasped in relief. San Francisco only led the game for the last ten minutes, but had tied the World Series.

The Game of My Life
By Rich Aurilia

We had been to the postseason before, with the same group of guys. We always felt that we would go deeper. Once we got past Atlanta in that first round, we felt vindicated.

After we saw Lackey a little bit in Game 2 and saw what kind of pitches he threw, it helped us facing him going into Game 4. For us, Woody got down early in the first few innings, and then after that he shut them down the rest of the way.

Down 3-0 into the fifth, I know I'll never forget the first two batters of that inning. Rueter led off and laid down a bunt that bounced off the plate, hit the grass, and spun. Lackey wasn't able to get a handle on it. Lofton was next and he laid down a bunt right on the foul line. It came back fair right when Glaus picked it up.

We had first and second, nobody out. That's when I came up and hit the base hit to right center. We came back and tied it that inning, and I ended up scoring the tying run.

That was a game I remember because we were on the brink of getting down, 3-1. It was exciting to come back late in the game and beat Frankie Rodriguez, who had been unhittable the whole month of September and all the postseason so far.

I was just happy we won the game. It was a great series to be involved in.

	1	2	3	4	5	6	7	8	9	R	H	E
Angels	0	1	2	0	0	0	0	0	0	3	10	1
Giants	0	0	0	0	3	0	0	1	x	4	2	1

Aurilia: 4 at-bats, 1 run, 3 hits, 1 double, 1 RBI, turned 3 double plays

---

Aurilia had a terrific postseason, hitting six homers and knocking in a team-high 17 runs, a record for a shortstop. It was the career pinnacle for the New York native who grew up playing stickball and breaking windows in an Italian neighborhood of Brooklyn. Aurilia worked hard to break into the Giants starting lineup in 1998 and to become an All-Star in 2001, hitting more home runs than any National League shortstop in 41 years. But hard work was nothing new to the son of a nurse and a stockroom worker, who moonlighted as a stage hand at the Metropolitan Opera while he was still a low-paid minor leaguer.

"He wasn't too flashy, he wasn't too outgoing. He was very consistent and very solid. I think that's what you look for in a shortstop," said Kent, Aurilia's teammate for six years. "His work ethic was impressive. He knew he wasn't one of the most gifted hitters out there, but he really worked to become a good one."

After San Francisco released the shortstop following the 2003 campaign, he played for Seattle, San Diego, and Cincinnati, hitting .300 for the 2006 Reds.

Then he returned to the Giants for three more years. After 11 seasons in orange and black, Aurilia retired among San Francisco's all-time leaders in batting average, runs, games, hits, doubles, RBIs and total bases.

"For me, San Francisco has always been home and a place where I love playing. This is where I spent most of my career and it's the place I wanted to finish my career," he said.

22

J.T. SNOW

"HOW I GOT IN THE HALL OF FAME"

POSITION: first base

SEASONS WITH GIANTS: 1997–2005

ACCOMPLISHMENTS: won Gold Gloves in 1997, 1998, 1999, and 2000; set Giants single-season record for fielding percentage by a first baseman (.999) in 1998; set Giants career record for a first baseman with .996 fielding percentage

GAME OF HIS LIFE: October 24, 2002 versus Anaheim Angels

LEAVE IT TO ONE of the greatest defensive first basemen of all time to make an unforgettable play on baseball's biggest stage. In Game 5 of the 2002 World Series, J.T. Snow saved his youngest teammate from disaster without even using his fabled glove.

"Thank God for J.T., who had the best hands in baseball," said the Giants' Shawon Dunston. "Somebody else would have dropped him, but J.T. made it look easy."

The highlight-reel moment that Snow shared with three-year-old batboy Darren Baker arrived near the end of the Giants home contest. San Francisco led the October 24 game early only to see the Anaheim Angels stubbornly strike back. In the first inning, Barry Bonds doubled home a run and Snow drew a walk in a three-run rally. After the Angels walked Bonds intentionally in the second, Benito Santiago knocked home two more runs with a single.

Reggie Sanders followed with a sacrifice fly that extended the Giants' lead to 6-0.

Yet San Francisco expected a fight, and Anaheim delivered one. Angels southpaw Jarrod Washburn recovered from his early struggles to pitch scoreless third and fourth frames. Meanwhile, the visitors tested San Francisco's Jason Schmidt with long at-bats that rapidly elevated the starter's pitch count. In the fifth, Anaheim sent eight men to the plate and capitalized on Schmidt's fatigue with a walk, four hits, and three runs. The Giants ace struck out eight batters that night but had already thrown 100 pitches. With two outs, manager Dusty Baker replaced him with reliever Chad Zerbe.

"I went out there and I tried to exert a little bit more when I had already been probably at my peak level," said Schmidt.

When the Angels' Bengie Molina singled, went to third on Benji Gil's double and scored on David Eckstein's infield out in the sixth, Anaheim crept within two runs.

"A lot of guys were swinging the bats pretty well. We didn't feel comfortable at all until we got up late in the game," Snow said. "We were up 6-0, they made it 6-4. They kept coming after us."

Emerging from a slump, Jeff Kent launched a two-run homer in the San Francisco sixth, so the Giants led by 8-4 when their first baseman led off the seventh. Snow ripped a line drive single up the middle past Anaheim pitcher Ben Weber. Next, the fireman hit David Bell with a pitch, moving Snow to second. Tsuyoshi Shinjo advanced both runners with a well-executed sacrifice bunt. Then Kenny Lofton lifted a high drive to right, setting into motion a unique and memorable event in World Series history.

Lofton's ball bounced off the wall for an easy extra-base hit. Snow ran home from third with Bell in hot pursuit. As he approached the plate, the first baseman suddenly saw another Giant running home. Darren, the skipper's son in a pint-sized batboy's uniform, was running into the play.

"Darren Baker was my little buddy in the clubhouse," explained Lofton. "He was always hanging around me and trying to do what I do. When I got

J.T. Snow's quick hands saved three-year-old Darren Baker from a potentially dangerous collision during Game 5 of the 2002 World Series. *AP Images*

a hit, he wanted to be the one to get my bat. I think that's what started this whole thing. One of the other batboys wanted to get it, so as soon as I hit it, Darren took off to beat him."

By the time his father saw him, it was too late to stop the youngster. "At three and a half, he could fly," the elder Baker said. "He was close to the plate already. I didn't know if he was going to slide in or what the heck was going on."

As Darren, Snow, and Bell converged on the plate—not to mention a baseball hurtling towards them from the outfield—fans in the ballpark held their breath, envisioning a collision that could seriously injure the littlest Giant. Snow handled the play as smoothly and as easily as if he'd practiced it since spring training. Just before the left-hander stepped on the plate, he reached out his right hand and grabbed Darren by his jacket. The Giant lifted the wide-eyed lad off the ground even as he scored. Then he carried him back to his stunned father in the dugout while Bell touched the plate behind them.

"He's got Gold Gloves for a reason," Dunston said with a laugh. "J.T. picked him clean like a ball in the dirt."

Baseball's detailed stenography had no shorthand for such an event: first baseman saves batboy, and two runs score. Snow's manager gave him a thankful high-five while the crowd and millions of viewers swooned.

"It happened so quick I didn't realize that he was in danger until J.T. had already moved him out of the way. Since then, I've seen so many replays of it," said Bell. "I'd like to believe I could have avoided him, but it was still a great heads-up thing that J.T. did. I think it helped that he's a dad. His instincts came out. It was a good moment."

Less pleased was the boy's father, who covered his face and shook his head, dreading the admonishments of his mother who worried that Darren was too young to be a batboy. Despite her concern, Dusty suited up his son because he wanted to spend every possible minute with him in the wake of his recent bout with cancer.

"I saw the play unfold, and I was thinking about what my mom told me. 'He shouldn't be out there. He's gonna get hurt,'" said Baker. "I said, 'Mom, I know what I'm doing.' First call I got back in the clubhouse was my mom to tell me, 'I know you listen to me sometimes. Just listen to me this time.' She told me to thank J.T." It caught Major League Baseball's attention, too. Before the 2003 season, baseball officials issued an order requiring batboys to be at least 14 years old. The edict became commonly known as the "Darren Baker rule."

In the game, however, the feel-good moment marked the end of the evening's worries and the beginning of a carefree World Series celebration. The flood gates opened and San Francisco scored six more times. Kent drilled another two-run homer in the seventh and Snow singled and scored again in the eighth. Rich Aurilia added a three-run blast, and San Francisco's bullpen gave the Angels nothing more. In their largest-ever postseason blowout, the Giants won, 16-4.

The Game of My Life
By J. T. Snow

I was on third, David Bell was on second, and Lofton hit that ball to deep right center. I went back to tag up because I wasn't sure the ball would fall in. I was watching the ball, and I believe David was halfway to third when it did fall in. So David was hustling while I'm running home.

I saw something come out of the dugout. I focused on it, and it was Darren. I thought he would stop, but he just kept going all the way to the plate. Right as he got there, Bengie Molina crouched down for a possible play, and the umpire tried to do something with his hand. I grabbed Darren, looked down, stepped on the plate, and then I lifted him up with one arm. I had so much adrenaline. David was right behind me, crossing the plate. Darren's eyes were just huge. I don't think he knew what was going on.

I'm thankful he didn't get hurt. It could have gotten ugly. I'm just glad that I held on and glad that his jacket didn't unbutton. It could have been a lot worse if I had dropped him or didn't get him or he got injured. Then people would look at it differently. I tell everybody that if they were in my shoes, they would have done the same thing. If you're a dad, you're used to chasing after kids now and then, and grabbing them by the jacket or shirt collar to keep them out of harm's way.

It was a big hit with all the moms. That's the one thing people always bring up. It's even in the Hall of Fame. Somebody told me he saw a picture of it in there. So that's how I got in the Hall of Fame.

	1	2	3	4	5	6	7	8	9	R	H	E
Angles	0	0	0	0	3	1	0	0	0	4	10	2
Giants	3	3	0	0	0	2	4	4	x	16	16	0

Snow: 4 at-bats, 2 runs, 2 hits, 1 walk

Darren was delighted to learn that his photo had reached Coopers–town. "I'm in the Hall of Fame!" the boy exclaimed. "No, you're not," his father told him, explaining the difference between induction into the shrine and merely having one's picture in the building. "He's constantly reminded of it by everybody he sees all over the world," said Baker. "People recognize me and then see him and say, 'Aren't you that kid?' He hears it everywhere."

With a rout in Game 5, the Giants took a 3-2 series lead and soaring hopes into the finale in Anaheim. San Francisco needed just one more win to clinch the 2002 World Series championship. In Game 6, the orange and black carried a 5-0 advantage into the seventh inning, and a 5-3 lead into the eighth, though many Giants players and fans would like to forget the conclusion of that contest and the series.

"We knew we were going to win that game," Aurilia said. "It was 5-0 in the seventh and we had our horses coming in, Felix Rodriguez, Tim Worrell, and Robb Nen. It was terrible the way we lost, but you've got to tip your hat to the Angels because they didn't give up. They kept coming at us and they beat our best guys out there. I'd trade every hit I had in that series to change the outcome."

The loss has lingered in the minds of many Giants, including Snow.

"It was very disappointing, heartbreaking," the first baseman said. "I still think about it all the time, being out there six outs away, thinking I was going to wear my ring everywhere and never take it off. Baseball is a crazy game. They came back and took it. It's tough thinking about what could have been."

Snow batted a robust .407 in the series, scoring six runs and knocking in four, collecting hits in each of the seven games. He ranks among San Francisco's all-time leaders in hits and walks, though he's best remembered for his many years of nonpareil defense. Snow's ability to field almost any ball hit his way constantly amazed fellow players and spectators. He won six Gold Gloves in his career, four of them in a Giants uniform. Snow owns the team records for fielding percentage in a career and in a single season, and that defensive prowess kept him in the lineup even when his offense began to wane.

"J.T. was such a phenomenal player," said Nen, Snow's longtime teammate. "It seemed like he made a diving catch in every game. He was just so solid. If it wasn't for him, all our ERAs would have been a lot higher."

Snow made it look easy, though there was nothing easy about becoming the best defensive first baseman the Giants ever had.

"I worked at it from the time I was a kid," he said. "My dad used to pound ground balls at me. There's no substitute for hard work and practice. I worked very hard at it, and I think it paid off. I always felt that defense was such an overlooked part of the game. Teams that are winning play great defense in any sport. I knew that over at first base, my defense could help the pitchers and win a lot of games."

San Francisco released the popular nine-year Giant after the 2005 season. After a short stint with the Boston Red Sox, he retired in 2006. Returning to the Bay Area, Snow settled in Hillsborough with his wife Stacie and son Shane. He's coached throughout the Giants organization and became a part-time broadcaster.

"It's still fun to be around the game," he said. "The broadcasters get to see a different side of it, which I enjoy."

Two years after he hung up his spikes, the Giants paid their former star a unique compliment. San Francisco signed Snow to a one-day contract for Sept. 27, 2008 and started him one last time at 24 Willie Mays Plaza. The first baseman suited up, took batting practice and trotted onto the field – only to find himself alone on the diamond. The other Giants stayed behind for a moment as a prank, and they weren't done. Teammates Rich Aurilia, Eugenio Velez and Omar Vizquel hurled him hard warm-up throws in the dirt. The Gold Glover picked them all clean.

"That was Omar's idea. He wanted to see if I still had it," said Snow with a laugh. "Luckily I made all the plays."

Before the first pitch, he left the game to high-fives and rousing cheers.

"That was a neat day," he said. "It felt good to officially retire as a Giant."

23

JASON SCHMIDT

"FOR MY MOM"

POSITION: pitcher

SEASONS WITH GIANTS: 2001–2006

ACCOMPLISHMENTS: All-Star in 2003, 2004, and 2006; led National League in ERA (2.34) in 2003; set San Francisco Giants single-season record for strikeouts (251) in 2004; tied team record with 16 strikeouts in a game in 2006; set San Francisco Giants career record for winning percentage (.678)

GAME OF HIS LIFE: April 30, 2003 versus Chicago Cubs

JASON SCHMIDT ALWAYS THREW hard, but on this particular day he even scared his catcher. From his first warm-up throws on April 30, 2003, the difference was unmistakable.

"I noticed (it after) about six or seven throws, and I knew it would be a special day for him," said Bill Hayes, the Giants bullpen catcher who warmed Schmidt up that day. "He was extra loose and pumped up, his adrenaline was rushing, and the thoughts of what he had been through the last ten days were all kind of bottled up. He had some lightning coming out while he was playing long toss."

Wearing a catcher's mask but no chest protector, Hayes felt especially vulnerable when he crouched behind the plate for his pitcher's warm-ups.

"The ball had some extra carry to it. I won't say I was petrified, but I was pretty alert," said Hayes. "A guy with his kind of arm strength, and me being almost 50 and having older eyes, I was hoping he wouldn't hit me in the chest. If one of those hit me in the heart, I probably wouldn't be here talking about it.

"About halfway through, I really wanted out of the whole situation," Hayes said. "After I got done, I said to myself, 'Okay, I survived that.' But I feared for those Cubs hitters."

Schmidt had every excuse to be off his game. Just ten days earlier, his mother, Vicki Schmidt, 53, had died of a cancer known as glioblastoma. Doctors had discovered a malignant brain tumor in March 2002 after Vicki experienced headaches and blacked out while driving. They operated and treated Vicki with chemotherapy, but offered little hope for her recovery.

"She was a person I called on the phone pretty much every single day," Schmidt said. "I don't want to say I was a mama's boy, but my parents divorced when I was young, and she was the one that raised me. She had the greatest impact on my life of anybody.

"I have one sister and three stepsisters," he said. "Her family was very large, too; she was one of seven kids. We had huge holidays. She was the glue that held everybody together."

Vicki took Jason to his first big league game at the Seattle Kingdome when he was nine. That's when he told her that one day he would play on such a field as a big leaguer himself. Twenty years later, Jason was a major league star, the Giants' ace, married and the father of a one-year-old girl. The news of Vicki's illness devastated the family, though she got to see him win a game in the 2002 World Series.

Schmidt got the call he had expected and dreaded for a year during the Giants early-season trip to Pittsburgh on April 22, 2003. His teammates consoled him while he cried in the clubhouse. San Francisco placed him on bereavement leave, and he flew to join his family in Longview, Washington. A game of catch with his brother-in-law in the street was the closest Schmidt came to a workout that week, but the 30-year-old pitcher looked anything but rusty upon rejoining the club. Possessed might be a better description.

Jason Schmidt smothered the Cubs in the game of his life, his first start after his mother died. *Lisa Blimenfeld/Getty Images*

"We all could see it from when he first got on top of the mound. You could tell he was different," said Dusty Baker, then in his first year managing the Chicago Cubs. "He was throwing about 95 or 97. His slider was nasty and his change-up was awesome. He was a man on a mission. You could tell he was going to be next to impossible to beat that night."

Schmidt retired the Cubs on eight pitches in the first inning. To the delight of over 40,000 fans, he struck out slugger Sammy Sosa with a 95-mph heater. He was perfect through three innings, retiring the first nine batters on 29 pitches with five strikeouts.

The Giants scored the only runs they would need in the second, when Benito Santiago singled in a run and Marquis Grissom knocked in another on a ground ball out. Barry Bonds smashed a two-run homer in the third, and homered again in the sixth, to stake San Francisco to a 5-0 lead.

Chicago had an opportunity in the fourth, loading the bases with two out as Mark Grudzielanek singled, Schmidt hit Moises Alou with a pitch, and then walked Hee Seop Choi. But the Giants ace crushed the rally by striking out Corey Patterson for one of three times on the night. Baker's boys never threatened again. Only once more did a Cub advance as far as second base, and never again did the visitors place two runners on base at once.

Schmidt finished with 12 strikeouts, still throwing 97 mph in the ninth as he retired Choi to end the game. The Giant threw a three-hitter on 117 pitches, and manager Felipe Alou, known for his quick hook, never so much as called the bullpen.

The Game of My Life
By Jason Schmidt

My mom contracted a brain tumor in spring training of '02, and they thought she had maybe six months to a year to live. She made it a little over a year.

I'd been off for ten days (prior to that game). I hadn't been in the bullpen or anything like that. While I was home, I grabbed my brother-in-law, and we played catch in the street by the house. I tried to stay home as long as I could, but I also wanted to get back on the field. I wanted to come back and make that start.

When I showed up at the ballpark, nobody said a word to me. Everybody knew where I had come from. For me, (pitching) was therapy. I was ready to get the most out of my therapy that day. I walked in and took my emotions out in the game.

I went out and warmed up, and it was like I had a cannon on me. It was the weirdest thing. I've never felt so strong in my life. I was hitting all the corners in the game. I thought, "Gosh, why do I feel so good?" I had a really big adrenaline rush.

Going out there, in my mind I knew no one was going to score off me. If we scored one run, that was all I needed. I don't mean that arrogantly or anything like that. It was just emotional. It was like somebody was with me on the mound that day.

	1	2	3	4	5	6	7	8	9	R	H	E
Cubs	0	0	0	0	0	0	0	0	0	0	3	0
Giants	0	2	2	0	0	1	0	0	x	5	6	0

Schmidt: win, 9 innings pitched, 3 hits, 0 runs, 2 walks, 12 strikeouts

---

Schmidt's game made a deep impression on his teammates, including his left fielder. Bonds called Schmidt's performance "incredible" and credited the pitcher's outing and a visit from his own cancer-stricken father as inspiration for his two home runs that night.

"Some of us have been going through some family personal things, but nothing more than what he went through," Bonds said of Schmidt. "That's big of him to come back as soon as he did and do what he did for us."

Agreeing with that assessment was Baker, the former Giants skipper who talked to Schmidt about his mother's illness and prayed for her.

"I hated that it was against us, but I understood, big time," said Baker, himself a cancer survivor, who managed Schmidt in San Francisco in 2001 and 2002.

"I was hoping he'd pitch a complete game. Everybody was pulling for him. It was very emotional for him and for everybody," said Felipe Alou. "We had a feeling like he was pitching for his mother. It was a special start for him."

Speaking to the press that night, a teary Schmidt called the game the highlight of his career.

"I went out there and tried to treat it like any other game," he told the writers. "I felt a little guilty going out there, not being home, but I'm glad I went out there. I said a little prayer before the game. I said, 'It's your will. Just give me this game tonight.' That was it."

Another baseball-savvy observer who found the game memorable was Henry Schulman, the Giants beat writer for the *San Francisco Chronicle*. "One thing I've found, and I've seen it a lot with Barry Bonds, is that the ball field almost becomes a sanctuary for players who are going through dire personal issues," said Schulman. "Bonds was able to hit two game-winning home runs the week his father died. I think players look forward to getting back on the field when something like that happens.

"It seemed to me that night that Jason had tunnel vision, where the only thing he was focused on was playing catch with the catcher, just getting the ball into the catcher's mitt. It was one of the best games that he ever threw as a Giant.

"I think he was a little surprised himself that he was able to go out there and throw that kind of game so soon after his mother died. Jason's a very religious man. He really does believe that there's an afterlife and that his mom who had suffered was in a better place. I think that was a comfort to him."

By the time Schmidt left San Francisco after the 2006 season, he had become a three-time All-Star. He pitched a complete-game shutout in the 2003 playoffs. He threw one-hitters against the Cubs and the Boston Red Sox in 2004. And in a masterful 2006 outing against the Florida Marlins, the hurler struck out 16 batters to tie the Giants' 102-year-old team record. Yet he says his most meaningful game remains his emotional win against the Cubs on April 30, 2003.

"That game was something that I felt like I did for my mom," he said.

24

BRIAN DALLIMORE

"A MAGICAL DAY"

POSITIONS: third base, second base

SEASONS WITH GIANTS: 2004–2005

ACCOMPLISHMENTS: set AAA Fresno Grizzlies record and led Pacific Coast League in batting average (.352) in 2003

GAME OF HIS LIFE: April 30, 2004 versus Florida Marlins

IN THE EARLY MOMENTS of the San Francisco's contest on April 30, 2004, there was no sign that a lifetime dream was about to wonderfully come true. In fact, an ugly loss in the making prompted groans throughout the ballpark.

With nine wins and 14 losses, the 2004 Giants occupied last place in the division, five games behind the Los Angeles Dodgers. It was a disappointing start for the team which easily won the National League West in 2003. And things weren't looking up for the Orange and Black on this night, either. Giants pitcher Kevin Correia got clobbered for nine runs in two innings, permitting three walks, six hits, and a home run. It would be Correia's first and last start of the season, and the worst appearance of his career. To make things worse, the team pounding the young right-hander was none other than the Florida Marlins, the same club had that knocked San Francisco out of the playoffs the previous October.

But while the game appeared discouraging, close observers of the team saw one point of interest: the arrival of a minor leaguer who'd been tearing up the Pacific Coast League. After second baseman Ray Durham pulled a hamstring, the Giants called up Brian Dallimore from their Class AAA affiliate, the Fresno Grizzlies. Minor league clubs don't typically employ farm hands already 30 years old, and big league teams promote them even less often. But Dallimore wasn't a typical minor leaguer. The infielder had won the Pacific Coast League batting championship in 2003, hitting .352, and when San Francisco called him up in 2004, he was batting a gaudy .375. The Giants' summons had been so sudden and unexpected that Dallimore had to fly to San Francisco without his gear. In fact, Dallimore had to scavenge items from teammates to suit up, playing in a pair of Neifi Perez's shoes and J.T. Snow's extra batting gloves.

Down 9-2 in the bottom of the second, the Giants managed to put some runners on base as Perez coaxed a walk, Yorvit Torrealba doubled to right, and Florida starter Dontrelle Willis hit Dustan Mohr with a pitch. Then Jeffrey Hammonds singled in a run, leaving the bases loaded as San Francisco trailed 9-3. Dallimore came to the plate against Willis, the 2003 All-Star and Rookie of the Year, with one goal in mind: score the run from third.

"I knew I had to put the ball in the outfield and get the run in," he said. "In my first at-bat, I walked on four pitches, so I got to see Willis' timing and the deception of his delivery. That helped settle me down a bit."

Willis threw a first-pitch slider. Dallimore swung and connected. The ball flew to left field, deep enough to score Torrealba from third, he thought.

"I remember distinctly saying to myself, 'Yes, sacrifice fly.' I'd done my job, I didn't make a mistake," he said. "That's what I was looking to do at that point. I knew I hit it okay." As he ran to first, Dallimore saw left fielder Wil Cordero turn his back to the infield and run for the fence.

Dallimore worked a long time to hit that fly ball. No player has an easy road to the majors, but Dallimore's was more difficult and longer than most.

Brian Dallimore's grand slam on April 30, 2004, was his only home run in the majors. *Lisa Blumenfeld/Getty Images*

The Las Vegas native and former Stanford star spent eight years toiling in the minor leagues in such places as Auburn, New York; Kissimmee, Florida; and Round Rock, Texas. By the time Dallimore began the 2004 season with the Fresno Grizzlies, he had played more than 800 minor league games all over the country. The one he remembers best, a 2001 contest he played for Arizona's Class AA team in El Paso, typifies the unglamorous nature of the minors.

"I was married for three years up to this point, and my in-laws had never seen me play pro ball," Dallimore said. "They came to watch us play for the weekend. It was funny because the game lasted 15 innings and I went 0-for-seven or -eight. They were practically falling asleep in the stands. Their first impression was not a very good one, though at the time I was doing pretty well in El Paso and we did actually win the game."

Kim Dallimore, Brian's wife, moved with him from one minor league town to another and attended hundreds of his games. The two met as children in Las Vegas when Brian played Little League with Kim's brother.

"We had the best of times but the hardest times, too, away from the family so much," said Kim. The couple's first child, Mandi, was born in 2001 after Brian's last season in El Paso. Then, it was on to Tucson for 2002.

Dallimore joined the Giants organization on December 16, 2002. His 2003 batting average of .352 not only led the Pacific Coast League but set a Fresno Grizzlies record. San Francisco's decision not to add him to their expanded September roster was heartbreaking, but he returned in 2004 anyway, determined to keep trying as long as he believed he had a chance to break through. That chance arrived on April 28 when the Giants ordered him to rush to San Francisco. He pinch-hit against the Braves the next day and grounded out.

One day later, manager Felipe Alou wrote him into the lineup at third base against Florida, batting second. The skipper's decision to start Dallimore surprised him. "I wasn't expecting to start at all, even more so in the two-hole, so I was excited and nervous all at the same time," he said.

Dallimore took batting practice that day in the same group as Barry Bonds, and the superstar didn't hesitate to remind the rookie who was who. "The second time I got in there, I hit six or seven balls, and Barry says, 'Get the f--k out of the cage, kid! Nobody's here to watch you. You're taking too many swings.' I just wanted to crawl under the mat. From then on I only took five pitches even though everyone else took eight."

Back in the clubhouse, Dallimore reflected on the many years he worked to reach his first big league start.

"Those two days were such a treat and so rewarding, it felt like it validated everything I'd been doing, even when people would look and say, 'Why are you still doing it?' and I felt like I wasn't getting a fair shake," Dallimore said. "I remember thinking that this in itself was a reward for all those hardships and all that time I spent, not knowing that it was only going to get better."

Dallimore's fly ball in the second inning sent Cordero to the wall. The Giant had already rounded first when he saw the left fielder look up at the ball sailing over his head. Only then did he realize this was no sacrifice fly. Dallimore had just clubbed a grand slam to bring the Giants back into the game.

In the stands, Kim and Brian's mother, Alice, shook with excitement. The two had raced from Reno to San Francisco when the team promoted Brian. Only shortly before the April 30 game did they learn that he was starting, so they raced again from their Fisherman's Wharf hotel to the park in time to see his big hit.

"I was in shock, absolutely flustered," admitted Kim. "I was so nervous, I didn't even know the bases were loaded. On the phone with my brother, I said, 'Brian just hit a three-run homer!' Then I found out it was a grand slam and I had to call him back." Alice's and Kim's cell phones both started ringing non stop as friends called to congratulate them.

Fred Dallimore, Brian's father, spent the day driving to Fresno to pick up his son's car and gear. Once an All-American pitcher and the head baseball coach at the University of Nevada Las Vegas for 23 years, Fred walked into the park just in time to see the ball clear the fence.

"It's neat to see a 30-year-old rookie hit a grand slam for his first hit," a fan remarked to him.

"Yeah, especially when he's your son," replied the beaming father.

An ecstatic group of Giants greeted him at the plate. The crowd stayed on its feet, roaring. Even Bonds slapped his hand as the slugger walked to the on-deck circle. In the dugout, relief pitcher Scott Eyre pulled Dallimore to an open seat beside him on the bench. "I want to get on TV," Eyre laughed. Dallimore sat panting, his heart still racing, in a state of disbelief. "Did this really just happen?" he asked himself.

But the game was far from over, and the Giants still trailed, 9-7. Dallimore's blow knocked Willis from the game, and Florida brought in Tommy Phelps to pitch. Then the rally continued as center fielder Marquis Grissom singled, Bonds walked, and Edgardo Alfonzo, playing second base, singled to load the bases again. Pedro Feliz, starting at first base, singled in Grissom and Bonds. Down seven runs just moments before, San Francisco had tied the game. Tyler Walker relieved Correia in the top of the third as the bullpen began seven innings of superb relief, allowing just three hits and no runs the rest of the way.

Dallimore singled to lead off the third, and singled again in the fifth, later to score on another Alfonzo hit. San Francisco took a 12-9 lead into the sixth inning when the Giant came to bat again. Then Marlins southpaw Matt Perisho plunked Dallimore on the thigh with his first pitch.

"I'd been hitting fastballs, hitting sliders, hitting curves, and feeling pretty good about it," he said. "I think it's an unwritten rule in the big leagues that when somebody gets off to a good start, you've got to unsettle him. He was sending a message: 'Don't get too comfortable.' It's all part of the game."

Dallimore turned his ankle while leaving the field that frame, so the Giants removed him in the eighth, moving Feliz to third and sending Snow to play first base. By then, the scoring was over. Giants closer Matt Herges finished the game with a perfect ninth inning.

Dallimore's line for the day was impressive: three hits in three at-bats, three runs, and four RBIs. With his walk and the beanball, he reached base five times in five plate appearances. The third baseman committed an error in the second, short-hopping a throw to first that Feliz couldn't handle. But later in the inning, he made a diving stop of a ground ball off the bat of Marlins catcher Mike Redmond to stop the Giants' bleeding.

After the game, a young man from the bleachers brought Dallimore's grand slam baseball to the San Francisco clubhouse. Dallimore offered to trade him a bat for the keepsake.

"Man, I don't want your wood," said the kid. "I want you and the Giants to fly me and my girlfriend out on a road trip with the team."

"Are you kidding me?" asked Dallimore.

"At least get us a couple of thousand dollars from the dugout store," the kid countered.

"You're talking to the wrong person," the rookie said.

But Dallimore got the ball eventually, or at least a ball. The league didn't exactly mark balls for his debut like it does for landmark Bonds homers, so he can't be entirely sure.

"The next day, the guy gives a ball to Jeffery Hammonds, and he gave it to me," Dallimore said. "As far as I know, it's the ball. It was more the memory that counts, anyway."

Dallimore's breakout game produced a pleasant dilemma for his skipper.

"He's quite a baseball player, and he put a big problem in my head," said Alou after the comeback. "I gotta find him a place to play him tomorrow after a night like that."

And so he did. Trainer Stan Conte sent Dallimore home with a device to simultaneously ice and move his sprained ankle all night. Ten hours later, Conte taped the ankle up tight and Dallimore took the field to start again at third.

"My second start in the big leagues, there was no way I was going to take myself out," Dallimore said. "(The injury) restricted my mobility and my speed a little bit, but as the days progressed, it got better."

Alou started Dallimore every day for the next week at either third or second base. But Durham's return from the disabled list a few weeks later spelled the end of the rookie's call-up. Dallimore would visit the big club a few other times in the next two years. He played a total of 27 major league games for the Giants in 2004 and 2005. Then he attended spring training with the Milwaukee Brewers in 2006, but did not make the team.

Faced with yet another year of Class AAA ball and uncertainty, Dallimore decided to retire, with 13 big league hits and a .260 average. The grand slam was his only home run in the majors.

The Game of My Life
By Brian Dallimore

I hit the home run off the end of the bat. I was totally shocked that it went that far. I had so much adrenaline that it probably gave me a little more bat speed.

As I stepped on home plate, I remember giving a big "Whoo hoo, let's get this party started!" There was so much excitement. I gave double high-fives to all three of my teammates standing there—Hammonds, Torrealba, and Mohr. Perez was on top of the dugout steps jumping up and down. I'll never forget that. He was as happy for me as I was. That was really cool.

Fox Sports gave us their video cut of the grand slam. The Marlins pulled Willis to bring in another pitcher, and the whole time, the cameras zoomed in on my family. They're all on the phone, all frantic, and my wife Kim is talking to her brother, telling him details. She was just in shock because the eight years in the minor leagues were the same for her as they were for me.

She's been through all the hardships. So that was just a great time for all of us, because we'd all been along for that long road.

You could have never dreamed of doing something like that, all those numbers across the board. It was just a wonderful day. Before I'd gotten up there, the team was struggling. It would have been easy to lose by ten runs in that game. Instead we had a huge comeback that sparked a little bit of life.

It's funny that in the last two or three years, for the little amount that I ever did in a Giants uniform, I probably get name recognition close to some guy who did five times that amount, all because of that first game.

	1	2	3		4	5	6		7	8	9		R	H	E
Marlins	4	5	0		0	0	0		0	0	0		9	9	1
Giants	2	7	0		0	3	0		0	0	x		12	16	1

Dallimore: 3 at-bats, 3 runs, 3 hits, 1 HR, 4 RBIs, 1 walk, 1 hit-by-pitch

---

After their slow start, the 2004 Giants won 91 games but failed to reach the playoffs, finishing behind the Dodgers in the final standings for the first time since 1996. Bonds matched and surpassed Willie Mays' 660 career homers on his way to his second batting title and seventh MVP award. But the April 30 game became a highlight not just for Dallimore and Giants fans but anyone who roots for a hard-working underdog.

"It's the story of an everyday guy who really wasn't supposed to make it, and got the opportunity and had a magical day," Dallimore said. "The media really latched on to it, which was cool, and it felt good for me, and the fans liked it. That makes it more special for me, because it's not just a moment for me but a moment for them as well."

The brevity of Dallimore's major league career saddens him, though he still considers his many years of effort worthwhile.

"I played well during my time at every level, and the fact that I'm done playing shows that somewhere there was a disconnect between my performance and getting an opportunity," he said. "I feel like I'm good enough to have played a long time in the major leagues.

"But there are things you can't control, and I believe things happen for a reason," Dallimore said. "I'm not bitter. I'm very fortunate for the memories I do have. I became a better person for it. That's what life boils down to."

Kim encouraged her husband to keep playing in 2006, but several factors played into Brian's decision to move on. The Dallimores had a second daughter, Melanie, about a year after his grand-slam game. Then, a few weeks after Opening Day in 2006, the couple had their third child, Brady, a boy.

Plus, Dallimore took a job in the gaming industry that didn't take him away from his wife and children for weeks at a time. Suddenly baseball didn't pull at him the same way anymore.

"I'm a 100 percent family man," Dallimore said. "Baseball is a glamorous lifestyle but there are a lot of hardships. This fits more with my values.

"One thing that saddens me the most is that Brady's not going to be able to see me play. That stinks," Dallimore said. "But I'm going to show him. He's going to get to see it on tape."

25

JONATHAN SANCHEZ

"HEAVEN"

POSITION: pitcher

SEASONS WITH GIANTS: 2006–

ACCOMPLISHMENTS: led National League pitchers in fielding percentage (1.000) in 2009; tied San Francisco record with seven consecutive strikeouts in 2010; led National League in hits per nine innings pitched (6.61) in 2010

GAME OF HIS LIFE: July 10, 2009 versus San Diego Padres

AS THEY PASSED THEIR fiftieth anniversary in San Francisco, the Giants faced a crossroads. Barry Bonds, their incomparable slugger and the face of the franchise for 15 years, left the team and the game. San Francisco suffered four straight losing seasons and missed the postseason six times in a row. Highly-paid free agents didn't produce as expected and the team increasingly looked to its young players to fuel a resurgence.

One of those was pitcher Jonathan Sanchez, 26, who faced a crossroads of his own. The southpaw from Puerto Rico with a mid-90s fastball, lively curve and tricky slider rose quickly through the Giants' organization after the 2004 draft. But the 2009 campaign saw opponents hammer him in game after game. With a 2-8 record, he was off to the worst start of his career.

As his losses mounted and his ERA grew to a gaudy 5.53, San Francisco removed him from the starting rotation. For three weeks, he labored in the bullpen as trade rumors swirled.

"He was wild and not making pitches he wanted to make, especially behind in the count," recalled pitching coach Dave Righetti. "It was a struggle for him. His breaking ball wasn't being very useful for him. So we worked with him on his delivery, on holding runners and not tipping pitches."

The intervention seemed to work. Sanchez pitched three innings over two bullpen outings without yielding a run. Then a bigger opportunity arrived when teammate Randy Johnson, the perennial All-Star and 300 game winner, tore his rotator cuff on July 5. To replace the Big Unit, the Giants brought Sanchez out of exile.

"I didn't want a second chance like that, with Randy getting hurt," Sanchez said. "But I had to take advantage of it."

Despite the strong relief appearances, the pitcher's confidence was shaky before the July 10 start against the Padres. "I didn't think I'd be out there very long," he admitted.

In fact, Sanchez made his own call for relief before the game, phoning his father in Puerto Rico. "Can you come and spend time with me for a little bit?" Sanchez asked his dad. "I just want you here to hang out with me. Don't worry about the money." So Sigfredo Sanchez flew to San Francisco in time to witness the most remarkable game of his son's career.

As it turned out, San Francisco would replace both ends of the battery that night. When catcher Bengie Molina joined his wife as she delivered their baby, the Giants placed Eli Whiteside behind the plate instead.

Before 30,298 fans at 24 Willie Mays Plaza, the two locked in right away. Sanchez induced a ground ball from Everth Cabrera and struck out Tony Gwynn Jr. and Kevin Kouzmanoff in the first. The southpaw followed up with harmless fly balls from Adrian Gonzalez, Chase Headley and Kyle Blanks in the second.

Sanchez's teammates did their part at the plate early and often. Infielders Travis Ishikawa, Edgar Renteria and Juan Uribe, center fielder Aaron Rowand and Whiteside contributed to a second inning rally that produced a four-run lead. Third baseman Pablo "the Panda" Sandoval belted a three-run homer in the fifth.

Meanwhile, Sanchez continued to stymie San Diego's offense frame after frame, looking little like the hittable pitcher who'd been pounded in the first half of the season. The pitcher showed excellent command, mixed his speeds and pitches and kept the Padres off balance.

"There's no question that getting first-pitch strikes and getting his breaking ball over the plate when behind in the count were huge factors," said Righetti. "When he went to his fastball, the hitters weren't on it because they had to respect the off-speed pitch. He wasn't just power pitching."

As the late innings arrived without a single Padre base runner, the fans began to whisper about the possibilities. No Giant had thrown a no-hitter since John "The Count" Montefusco in 1976. None had achieved the feat in San Francisco since Ed Halicki in 1975.

"He had great stuff that night and I had the best seat in the house," said Whiteside. "Around the seventh inning, I realized they didn't have any hits, and nobody had even been on base. But it's still pretty tough to go three innings without allowing a hit in a big league ballgame."

After every out, the fans cheered louder. When the southpaw struck out the side in the seventh, they roared.

Gonzalez, San Diego's best hitter, flew out to lead off the eighth. Then Headley hit a slow grounder to third. Uribe tore after it but couldn't field it cleanly and the Padres had their first base runner at last. But the scorekeeper ruled the play an error. The no-hitter was still intact.

"I went out there after that play to talk to him and slow things down," Whiteside recalled. "When something happens in a game like that, you want to step back and take a deep breath."

Jonathan Sanchez pitched the Giants' first no-hitter in 33 years. *Dan Johanson*

Pitching from the stretch for the first time, Sanchez shook off the setback and retired pinch hitter Craig Stansberry on a fly ball and struck out Eliezer Alfonzo.

After Rowand knocked home a final insurance run in the eighth, Sanchez climbed the hill in the top of the ninth, three outs away from history. He got the first when Luis Rodriguez grounded out to short, setting off a loud cheer from a delighted crowd.

Edgar Gonzalez, the next batter, provided considerably more drama. When the Padre drilled a ball deep to center, hearts sank throughout the ballpark. But a sprinting Rowand caught the ball and held it even as he collided into the fence, showing every bit of the gritty determination for which he's known. Fans leaped out of their chairs and shouted in wild elation.

"I was going to go up and over and land on the other side of the fence, if I had to, to make a catch," said the center fielder.

"I thought it was gone, a home run," Sanchez said. "Rowand did a hell of a job to grab that ball." This was the moment when Sanchez said he first thought about the feat he had nearly accomplished, even if everyone watching had thought of nothing else for several innings. "When you get a play like that, you've got to get the no hitter," he said.

With two down, San Diego's last hope was Cabrera. The shortstop battled the pitcher to a 2-2 count. Then Sanchez uncorked a curve, the same pitch he failed to master in his early-season funk. The ball snapped over the plate into Whiteside's glove: strike three called.

Hours before, Sanchez had been talented but tattered and perhaps nearing the end of his San Francisco tenure. Now the shy and modest Giant was the first pitcher to throw a no-hitter for the orange and black in 33 years. His teammates mobbed him on the diamond. Delirious fans screamed their approval long after the last pitch, many of them shouting "Felicidades!" The stirring theme of "The Natural" rang throughout the park.

But the aftermath of this game offered another scene even more memorable. Sigfredo Sanchez, who flew in just the night before and had never seen Jonathan start a major league game, joined the Giants in the dugout. As father and son held a long embrace, they weren't the only ones fighting back tears.

The Game of My Life

By Jonathan Sanchez

I was having trouble getting my pitches over the plate that year. The only pitch I was throwing was the fastball because I couldn't get my breaking ball over for strikes. People were sitting on my fastball. You can't get big league hitters out that way.

When they put me in the pen, I started working on my windup. I got on top of the ball better. I started to throw the breaking ball for strikes and get people out without using the fastball so much. I wanted to be a starter and they gave me a second chance.

I was just keeping the ball down, throwing my pitches. Everything Eli called, I threw, even things I wasn't throwing for a strike. He put his fingers down and said, "You've got to throw it." I had to trust my stuff. He did an amazing job and everybody made good plays.

I wasn't thinking about it the no-hitter until Rowand caught that ball. Then I fought with the last guy to get him out.

It was amazing, the jubilation, all the fans cheering, everybody celebrating every pitch and enjoying every moment. When I threw the last pitch, I had goose bumps. Then my teammates were all over me. I thought, did this happen for real? I'm so proud that my dad was there with me.

When you're pitching well, going deep into games and giving the team a chance to win, everyone's proud of you. But to throw a no-hitter, you've got to do it to know what that feels like. You feel like you're in heaven.

God knows what he's doing. He put me in the pen for a reason, and it worked out.

	1	2	3	4	5	6	7	8	9	R	H	E
Padres	0	0	0	0	0	0	0	0	0	0	0	1
Giants	0	4	0	0	3	0	0	1	x	8	12	1

Sanchez's no-hitter proved significant far beyond July 10. The pitcher who had never even thrown a complete game before finished the season on a tear. With five more wins in the final months, he reduced his walks, increased his strikeouts and lowered his ERA by more than a point.

"From that day on, whether I was ahead or behind in the count, I was usually able to throw the breaking ball for a strike," he said.

Likewise, the Giants heated up with 88 wins in 2009, a 16-game improvement over 2008. Sanchez and his teammates built upon that success in 2010 to a greater degree than most imagined possible.

26

JEREMY AFFELDT

"AN AMAZING RIDE"

POSITION: pitcher

SEASONS WITH GIANTS: 2009–

ACCOMPLISHMENTS: led National League relief pitchers in ERA (1.73) and double plays (18) in 2009, set a San Francisco record for holds (33) in 2009

GAME OF HIS LIFE: October 23, 2010 versus Philadelphia Phillies

---

IN "THE CITY OF BROTHERLY LOVE," the Giants were getting anything but.

Emotions ran hot on October 23, 2010, even before Giants pitcher Jonathan Sanchez drilled Phillies second baseman Chase Utley with a fastball. The hit was clearly unintentional, giving the Phillies runners on first and second in a tied game with the pennant on the line, but the home fans jeered nonetheless. Then they furiously erupted after Utley threw the ball at Sanchez, the pitcher angrily shouted at him and both clubs stormed the field.

In San Francisco's bullpen, pitcher Jeremy Affeldt started to run toward the wild melee with his teammates. Then he felt a hand grab his shirt.

"You can't go out there!" bullpen coach Mark Gardner shouted over the deafening crowd. "You stay here. You need to lock it in right now. You're coming into this game!"

So while every other uniformed player mobbed the diamond for a shouting match and maybe more, Affeldt returned to the bullpen mound to warm up and face the undivided wrath of Phillies fans who unleashed a torrent of vile and unprintable insults at him.

That moment in Philadelphia was a turning point in a season full of them for the orange and black. The 2010 season saw San Francisco return to the postseason for the first time since Barry Bonds departed, relying instead on a roster of "castoffs and misfits," as the press called them. Indeed, the new Giants got surprising production from many unlikely sources.

Andres Torres, a 32-year-old outfielder, had never played in more than 59 games before joining the Giants and becoming a star leadoff hitter. Tim Lincecum, the paper-thin pitching phenom known as "The Freak," continued to amaze the baseball world with his whip-like delivery and pinpoint command. In contrast, third baseman Pablo Sandoval nearly won a batting title the previous season despite his chunky physique that made him known as "The Kung Fu Panda." And San Francisco reaped great dividends from veterans whose old teams had simply discarded them, like Juan Uribe, Pat Burrell, Aubrey Huff, Cody Ross, Edgar Renteria and also Affeldt.

A playoff race for the ages came down to the last day of the season. With five shutout innings and a surprising triple from their pitcher Sanchez, key hits from first baseman Huff, second baseman Freddie Sanchez and rookie catcher Buster Posey, and four innings of nearly perfect bullpen relief, the Giants eliminated the Padres and clinched their first National League West title in seven years.

"My heart was racing a thousand miles an hour," said Huff, who played ten seasons on losing teams before joining the Giants in 2010. "To finally get in after all those years, I'd never felt an emotion like that."

In the Division Series against the Braves that followed, most Giants saw the first postseason action of their careers. San Francisco eliminated Atlanta in four hard-fought, nail-biting games each decided by a single run.

The baseball fever that struck Northern California during these events rivaled any in the region's history. Sandoval-inspired "Panda" hats, long-

Jeremy Affeldt shut down a fearsome Phillies rally with the National League pennant on the line. *Dan Johanson*

haired wigs styled after Lincecum's stringy locks and faux black beards in tribute to pitchers Sergio Romo and Brian Wilson all appeared in droves. But both the fans' enthusiasm and the team's success only previewed greater things to come.

In the National League Championship Series, the upstart Giants faced a Phillies team that earned baseball's best regular season record in 2010, armed with ace pitcher Roy Halladay and fearsome power hitters like Ryan Howard. National pundits gave the Giants little chance to prevail.

Splitting the first two games in Philadelphia, the Giants won the third and fourth at 24 Willie Mays Plaza. But the Phillies struck back in Game 5, forcing a return to Citizens Bank Park. Still leading the series, 3-2, the Giants had their work cut out for them to beat the reigning league champions again, especially in a city unmatched in baseball for its loud hostility toward visitors. The home crowd needed no encouragement but got some anyway from Phillies manager Charlie Manuel.

"Let 'em have it," the skipper ordered the Phaithful. "Let. Them. Have. It. All of them. For real!"

When Affeldt turned away from the fracas to prepare himself in the bullpen, that's exactly what they did.

"They challenged my manhood a dozen different ways," recalled the Giant. "I was the only guy in the pen, and there were a lot of fans who were really roasting me and letting me have it. Philadelphia is maybe the worst in baseball when it comes to hostile situations like that."

Affeldt, 31, was no stranger to the adversity that relief pitchers face in close games. The fireman from Spokane, Washington, was then a nine-year journeyman who'd also played for Kansas City, Colorado and Cincinnati. With San Francisco in 2009, he led all National League relievers with a 1.73 ERA and 18 double-play grounders, winning honors as setup man of the year. But a strained oblique forced him onto the disabled list on July 24, 2010. He saw limited action for the rest of the regular season and did not play in the Division Series.

"In September the team has to go with who's hot and who's working," Affeldt said. "We had guys like Javier Lopez and Ramon Ramirez who were doing a great job, so it was hard for me to get back into it. I wasn't able to do much, which was frustrating."

Affeldt would never get a bigger opportunity to help his club than the third inning of Game 6. When manager Bruce Bochy called him in to replace Sanchez, the Phillies had two men on base, nobody out and a ballpark full of momentum in their favor. At the plate was the slugging first baseman Howard, MVP of the 2006 season and the 2009 NLCS. Tied 2-2, the game and the series could turn on a single pitch.

Affeldt snapped a curveball over the plate for a called strike one. Howard fouled off an inside fastball for strike two. After two heaters low and away, Affeldt fired another 93-mph fastball above the zone. Howard swung through it for a huge first out.

"That was most critical," Affeldt said. "Howard is obviously a really dangerous player, and because there were no outs, you need to get him out without advancing the runners. Then the next guys have to do more than just hit a sacrifice fly."

Next Affeldt dueled with Philadelphia's right fielder Jayson Werth for eight pitches, finally retiring him on a fly ball to right. Then the pitcher shot a fastball inside to Shane Victorino. The center fielder grounded weakly to first, where Huff corralled the ball and won a footrace to the bag to end the scoring threat.

"That stadium was rocking as loud as I've ever heard," said Posey. "We had to find a way to kill the momentum there. Jeremy came in and did just that. For him to come in and get those huge outs, that was unreal."

After the Giants failed to score in the top of the fourth, Affeldt returned to pitch another frame. He started by inducing an easy grounder to short from left fielder Raul Ibanez. Catcher Carlos Ruiz struck out on a fastball over his shoes. Then pitcher Roy Oswalt sprayed a ball to right that found the glove of Ross. Retiring all six men he faced, Affeldt had quieted a perfect Philadelphia storm.

The southpaw's clutch play ranks among the game's greatest performances in the essential yet unappreciated field of middle relief pitching.

Many other Giants delivered indispensible contributions in a breathtaking game that remained precarious until the last pitch. That was only appropriate from a team that seemed to produce a hero a game, and sometimes a hero an inning, all year long.

San Francisco needed a needed a miracle to hold the hard-hitting Phillies scoreless from that point in their batting-friendly ballpark. A team built on stellar pitching tried its best to deliver one. Following Affeldt's outing, rookie starting pitcher Madison Bumgarner took the ball and calmly retired Philadelphia in the fifth and sixth. Lopez followed with a perfect seventh.

Then with two outs in the Giants' eighth, Uribe stepped to the plate. The third baseman with a knack for timely hits pounced on Ryan Madson's hanging slider, launching a ball the opposite way that barely cleared the right field fence. In the stands, most of the 46,062 red-clad fans fell into stunned silence. But Uribe and his jubilant teammates celebrated their 3-2 lead, six outs from the World Series.

"Everybody was excited when he hit that shot, especially because he hit the ball the other way," Affeldt said. "I don't think it could have come at a better time."

Bochy summoned Lincecum as setup man, and The Freak struck out Werth to start the Phillies' eighth. But when the home team rallied with singles by Victorino and Ibanez, Wilson entered the game to attempt an extra-hard save that strained hearts throughout the orange and black nation. Ruiz hit a line drive towards right field that could have tied the game. Instead, Huff snared it and threw to second for a double play. The thrilling play ended the inning, yet the All-Star closer would fight another battle in the ninth.

After San Francisco failed to score in the top half, Wilson retired two batters while the relentless Phillies fought back with two walks. Howard came to bat with a chance to win the game. The two dueled to a full count. Finally,

Wilson hurled a cutter towards the lower corner away from the slugger, who let it pass. An instant later, the umpire called an emphatic strike three.

For the fourth time in their San Francisco history, the Giants had won the pennant and an exuberant celebration began on the field in Philadelphia and at their home, 3,000 miles away.

The Game of My Life
By Jeremy Affeldt

When there's a fight and your brother's out there, you've got to make sure you're defending him. I tried to go but Gardy hogtied me in the bullpen and made me warm up. That was awkward but I think it ended up working out for me. I was able to concentrate on what I needed to do and I felt loose and at peace when I entered the game. The fans were saying a lot of mean things to me but I was so focused in that situation that they didn't seem that loud. If I let a distraction like that affect me, that would tell me that I'm not ready to go into that game.

In Philly there's a short porch in left field and in right field. If you hit it right, it's going to go. So we tried to prevent them from getting a majority of the bat head on the ball, stay out of their zones and keep them off balance to eliminate their power.

Posey and I were on same page. I didn't shake him off one time. It was the best I'd felt since I came back from my oblique injury. I'm glad it came together at the right time.

We held off a pretty good offense and scored key runs against strong pitching. To clinch it in that game was huge for us. It made all the difference in the world. With the kind of lineup Philadelphia had and the way we used our pitching in Game 6, I don't think anyone would have given us much chance to win Game 7 in Philly, though anything could have happened.

The crowd got quiet in a hurry. They weren't real happy about it. But we all felt like champions that night. It was awesome.

	1	2	3	4	5	6	7	8	9	R	H	E
Giants	0	0	2	0	0	0	0	1	0	3	13	0
Phillies	2	0	0	0	0	0	0	0	0	2	8	1

Affeldt: 2 innings pitched, 0 hits, 0 runs, 0 walks, 2 strikeouts

---

As the players reveled in a champagne shower, Bochy reflected on the club's hard-won glory.

"Not bad for a bunch of castoffs and misfits," the smiling skipper said. "When you get a group of guys all trying to accomplish the same thing, pulling together and playing with a lot of heart, you can see what happens. We had to beat a terrific team."

To defeat the heavily favored Phillies in the final game, the Giants played 18 of their 25 men. Lopez got the win, Uribe scored the winning run, Wilson got the save, and Ross was named the series MVP. But the team's brass gave Affeldt special recognition.

"I'm most proud of Jeremy. To me, he was the game," said pitching coach Dave Righetti.

"Affeldt saved us," Bochy agreed.

A married father of two children, Affeldt has applied himself to more than just baseball. He lent his name and support to the Not For Sale campaign, which combats human trafficking, and started his own youth ministry called Generation Alive. These community-minded efforts failed to stop Phillies fans from berating him loudly enough to crack the Liberty Bell again but Affeldt holds no grudge.

"We were just excited about winning and going to the World Series," he said with a smile. "It was an amazing ride."

Thrilling as it was, the ride was not over.

"We jumped around as a team and celebrated but I understood that had been done before. I allowed myself to feel good about it for 15 minutes," Wilson said. "The bigger challenge was still ahead so then I started preparing and thinking about the World Series."

27

BRIAN WILSON

"OUR YEAR"

POSITION: pitcher

SEASONS WITH GIANTS: 2006–

ACCOMPLISHMENTS: All-Star in 2008 and 2010; led National League and tied Giants single-season record in saves (48) in 2010

GAME OF HIS LIFE: November 1, 2010 versus Texas Rangers

DURING THE GIANTS' FIRST 53 years in San Francisco, they showed their fans almost everything baseball has to offer.

From Willie Mays to Tim Lincecum, the team boasted some of the game's brightest stars. Pitchers threw no-hitters and won Cy Young awards; Mike McCormick did both. Brimming with youth and promise, Willie McCovey, Gary Matthews, John Montefusco, and Buster Posey won Rookie of the Year awards. Barry Bonds broke home run records.

For 40 years, fans shivered in the game's coldest confines at Candlestick Park. Then they reveled in the nation's finest ballpark at 24 Willie Mays Plaza. They saw their club lose 100 games in 1985 and cheered the winners of four National League pennants. But heartbreak struck after the first three, each more painful than the last, and no city in baseball history had ever waited so long to win its first world championship.

San Francisco earned a chance to change that history on Nov. 1, 2010, thanks to contributions from every player on the roster. For instance, fleet

228

Brian Wilson recorded the final outs for San Francisco's first World Series championship. *Dan Johanson*

footed Darren Ford didn't appear in the playoffs but helped deliver essential wins as a pinch runner in the regular season. Outfielder Cody Ross, on the other hand, barely played until October when he blasted five home runs and ten RBIs.

"That was the beauty of our team," said closer Brian Wilson. "We never counted on one player to do it all. There was always another guy ready to step up. We had heroes from every position. Every game was perfectly won."

Still, the 2010 Giants would have gone nowhere without the strength of their pitching, especially their home-grown arms. Tim Lincecum, Matt Cain, Jonathan Sanchez, Madison Bumgarner and Wilson, who each came up through San Francisco's farm system, led a staff that posted the most strikeouts and best ERA in baseball, even shutting out playoff opponents four times.

In particular, the 28-year-old Wilson lifted his team in a career year. With 48 saves, the All-Star led baseball and tied Rod Beck's team record. He finished off the Padres as the Giants clinched the playoffs, earned two saves in the Division Series followed by three saves and a win in the ferocious National League Championship Series.

That success plus a colorful personality made him a fan favorite. When his bright orange game shoes led to a $1,000 league fine, he laughed off the penalty for "too much awesome on my feet" and blackened the offending footwear with a pen. His creative grooming, from his Mohawk to the scruffy facial hair he grew in 2010, drew countless smiles and imitators. "Fear the Beard!" became a popular slogan on signs and t-shirts. Yet the New Hampshire native showed a serious side after every save with a cross-armed gesture to honor God and his father, who died of cancer when Wilson was 17.

Winning three of the first four contests against the Texas Rangers in the 2010 World Series, San Francisco stood one game away from baseball's greatest prize. Even so, the Giants faced a formidable opponent in starting pitcher Cliff Lee, an All-Star who threw seven complete games in 2010. San

Francisco countered with Lincecum in a pitching duel worthy of the Fall Classic.

Lee allowed the Giants just three hits and no runs in the first six innings. "The Freak" matched him frame for frame, holding Texas scoreless on two hits. A capacity crowd of 52,045 at Rangers Ballpark in Arlington, including team owner Nolan Ryan and former President George W. Bush, held its collective breath. Texas had just won its only American League pennant and, like San Francisco, fought for its first World Series championship.

In the seventh, the Giants finally mustered a threat. With singles by Ross and Juan Uribe, they put two runners on base for the first time. A surprising bunt by Aubrey Huff, the first of his 11-year career, advanced them to second and third. After Lee struck out Pat Burrell, it appeared the Rangers would escape the jam. To preserve the tie, they had only to retire Edgar Renteria.

Renteria had delivered a World Series winning hit for the Florida Marlins in 1997, but the soft-spoken shortstop had largely disappointed himself and Giants fans with two injury-filled years in San Francisco. Yet he came alive in the 2010 Fall Classic with a home run, three RBIs, five runs and six hits in the first four games.

"We felt good with Edgar out there," said manager Bruce Bochy. "He'd shown a knack for getting the big hit."

A big hit was needed in the scoreless game. Lee's first pitch missed high, as did his second. For a moment, it appeared he would walk the batter. But when the third pitch caught the middle of the strike zone, Renteria pounced. The shortstop drove a ball towards left center that seemed to carry well. Outfielders Josh Hamilton and David Murphy raced to make a catch. Shockingly, the ball flew over them and the wall. Months before, Renteria had considered retiring mid-season but now he'd smashed a three-run homer that brought the Giants to the brink of a championship.

"I was hurt all year, but I kept myself in shape, kept working hard and kept telling myself, 'Be patient,'" Renteria said. "I had confidence in myself. He put a cutter straight over the middle and that's what I wanted."

Pumped-up players exchanged hugs and high-fives in the Giants dugout while millions of Bay Area fans went berserk in bars and family rooms. Yet Texas right fielder Nelson Cruz fired back with a solo shot that made the score 3-1.

"I didn't forget that we were playing a great offensive team," Renteria said. "That's why I told my teammates, 'Keep playing hard.' We knew they could tie the game right away."

The game remained tight when Bochy summoned Wilson in the ninth, a move that surprised some only because the starter was pitching so well.

"I thought Lincecum was going to go all nine, but they brought me in," Wilson said. "I couldn't blow that game after they showed that confidence in me."

San Francisco frequently called on Wilson to finish close games from the eighth inning with men on base, a feat he accomplished ten times in the 2010 regular season, more than any other pitcher. Entering the ninth inning of Game 5 with a two-run lead was a rare luxury although the Giants knew to take nothing for granted. Wilson had pitched the most innings of his career that season even before reaching the playoffs.

"When you're in the playoffs for the first time, there are no excuses," the Giant said. "The last thing you want is your team to think you're tired."

Wilson looked anything but tired as he struck out Hamilton to open the frame. The center fielder took a 95-mph heater for called strike three and shook his head as he walked back to the bench. Then designated hitter Vladimir Guerrero grounded out on one pitch.

Cruz stepped to the plate representing the Rangers' last hope and the Giants' last obstacle. If Wilson felt the pressure of the situation, he showed no sign.

"He likes that intensity," Lincecum said of his teammate. "He likes to have the game on his shoulders."

Throwing his trademark cutters and 96-mph fastballs, Wilson ran the count full. Finally he hurled a heater high and inside. Cruz swung right through it.

Wilson barely had time to make his customary cross-armed gesture before a mad throng of delirious players mobbed him on the mound. There had been dogpiles on the diamond and champagne showers before but nothing compared to this. Meanwhile, an unprecedented outburst of euphoria broke out in Northern California. Long-suffering fans who endured Candlestick for decades, others who latched onto the team at 24 Willie Mays Plaza and even toddlers wearing orange and black and sporting Wilson-esque beards exalted in joy. The San Francisco Giants had won their first World Series.

The Game of My Life
By Brian Wilson

Our pitching staff and our position players, we all came together. We had a bunch of team effort guys, coming up big in late-inning situations, getting two-out hits, striking out the lefty. Everybody made a huge contribution. I was never part of a team like that before. When we made the playoffs and won the pennant, I was really happy for the team and for the city. But we were out to win the World Series. It would have been such a shame if we'd lost because it was clearly our year.

What a battle it was leading up to that moment. Edgar Renteria nailed it. Lincecum, our ace, showed dominance on the mound. He was the guy we wanted out there.

You can deal with the pressure of closing in one of two ways. You can either be the hero or be the loser. Obviously I don't choose the latter. My role is one tiny key element towards a nine inning baseball game. Still, all eyes are on you in that moment. The only way to get through that is to be comfortable in your own skin.

I've got a fastball and then a cutter. Those are my strengths. I work them in and out, up and down. That's it. If you execute your pitches and throw them where you want to throw them, it's going to work out. In that situation, it did.

I could never imagine how it would feel. We didn't even know what we were supposed to do. Were we supposed to dogpile? Instead we danced around like a bunch of kids. It was an amazing feeling. I loved every minute of it.

	1	2	3	4	5	6	7	8	9	R	H	E
Giants	0	0	0	0	0	0	3	0	0	3	7	0
Rangers	0	0	0	0	0	0	1	0	0	1	3	1

Wilson: save, 1 inning pitched, 0 hits, 0 runs, 0 walks, 2 strikeouts

---

Renteria became just the fourth player to deliver game-winning hits in two Fall Classics. With his .412 batting average, six RBIs and surprising defensive play, he was an easy choice for the World Series MVP award.

From the postseason's start to finish, however, Wilson contributed as much as any Giant. In 11.2 innings pitched, he allowed just five hits, four walks, struck out 16 and posted a perfect 0.00 ERA.

"He may very well have been the MVP of October," broadcaster Duane Kuiper said.

San Francisco pulled out all the stops for its long-awaited championship parade, attended by an estimated million people. Players, coaches, broadcasters and team executives riding in convertibles and cable cars followed the exact route of the team's 1958 welcome parade. Bochy escorted the Commissioner's Trophy. Smiling faces extended as far as the eye could see. Ticker tape rained from the sky. Hours of boisterous cheering left ears aching all over town.

"Now every baseball team in the world knows why you fear the beard!" joked Governor Arnold Schwarzenegger at the victory ceremony. The crowd laughed while Wilson pumped his fist.

"The parade was complete chaos and the single greatest moment of my life," Wilson said. Because the Giants clinched on the road, it was the first opportunity for the players to celebrate with their faithful supporters. "We weren't the only ones who won a world championship," he said. "The fans did too."

No one captured the historical context and the fans' happy relief better than newspaper columnist Carl Steward, himself a Giants supporter since the early 1960s.

"It is unlikely any of the 2010 Giants can comprehend the massive exorcism they have performed for their older fans: the release from 52 years of mixed baseball memories in San Francisco," Steward wrote. "The shackles of lifelong disillusionment and disappointment are finally unbound… I can die happy now."

The columnist related a litany of crushing disappointments, such as McCovey's line drive that could have won the 1962 World Series but instead found the glove of Yankees second baseman Bobby Richardson. Another was San Francisco's second World Series spoiled by the 1989 Loma Prieta earthquake. Scott Spiezio's three-run homer that helped the Anaheim Angels turn around the 2002 World Series made the list, as did J.T. Snow's out at home that ended the Giants 2003 playoff run.

"Today, it's as if McCovey's line drive finally went through. And the earthquake didn't happen. And Spiezio struck out. And Snow was safe," Steward wrote. "Giants fans finally are free and fulfilled, liberated from 52 years of titleless infamy in San Francisco."

AFTERWORD

A HANDMADE WOODEN SCOREBOARD adorns the wall of my classroom at Castro Valley High School. On it, students and I post the scores from all San Francisco Giants wins – but never losses. The kids like it and the winning tallies comfort me on tough days. I love what I do but all teachers need to turn their minds to other things sometimes.

Baseball became a much bigger diversion for me when I began this book about the Giants. Juggling these duties wasn't always easy; sometimes I felt like a pitcher forced to divide his attention between a dangerous batter and a speedy base runner. But as a writer and lifelong baseball fan, I couldn't pass up the opportunity to put my stamp on the Giants' greatest games.

Getting to know the players was exciting and fun. Most were happy to talk about their favorite contests. Felipe Alou, Dave Dravecky, Tito Fuentes, Mike Krukow, Robby Thompson, Kirk Rueter, Robb Nen and Darren Lewis were especially helpful. By far the most animated was the friendly Brian Dallimore, still full of enthusiasm about his dreamy debut start. A writer must pay dues before the Giants grant him a date with Willie Mays, so after months of lobbying, it was rewarding to sit down with the "Say Hey Kid." Interviewing Barry Bonds was another memorable challenge. It was hard to catch him in a good mood but when I approached him in his clubhouse recliner, he shared recollections of a few teammates.Some players took months to contact, and some that I very much wanted to include could not be found or persuaded to contribute. But I was encouraged to find Giants from each of the decades since the club moved to San Francisco, including many who don't get much ink anymore like Bobby Bolin, Al Gallagher and Don Robinson.

As far as I know, this book contains the last interview of Rod Beck, who died in 2007. It was an honor, "Shooter."

The Giants' astonishing 2010 World Series win provided a perfect ending just in time for the book's second edition, not to mention validating the faith and loyalty of San Francisco fans dating back to 1958. At last I could place a world championship pennant next to that scoreboard in my classroom, although I had golden memories even before the Giants won their golden trophy. This book helped me rekindle them. I hope it does the same for readers.

ACKNOWLEDGMENTS

"It's Giants baseball. Anything can happen," was once a San Francisco marketing slogan. But this book would not have happened, nor even come close, without clutch hits from players at all levels of the game.

For kindly sharing their time and memories, warm thanks to the San Francisco players who make up the roster of this collection.

I'm grateful to these helpful members of the Giants organization, my starting lineup for facilitating access and interviews: Peter Magowan, Pat Gallagher, Matt Hodson, Blake Rhodes, Maria Jacinto, Jim Moorehead, Becky Biniek, Shirley Casabat and Bertha Fajardo.

For help in copy editing, research and photography, thanks to these up-and-coming stars: Bianca Arias, Gray Bae, Ellen Yau, Dawn Berden, Malena Bell, Laura Mitchell, Ariel Navarro, Flora Tsang, Mari Robinson, Christina Cross, Kamry Zhang, Tim Buhlig, Adam Andrie, and Chris Hongzhe Qian.

All-Star honors go to Tom Johnson, Len Sellers, Erna Smith, Dave Buscema, Doug Hoepker, John Humenik, Bruce Macgowan, Terri Bucklin, Morry Angell, Carl Steward, Elaine Ernst-Stall, Larry Duckwall and the System Reference Center of the Alameda County Library for assistance, inspiration and encouragement.

Most importantly, I'm grateful to my Hall of Fame-worthy family members and friends who supported my work on this project even though it kept me from spending time with them. Karen Johanson, Tom Johanson, Diane Johanson, Dan Johanson, Steve Johanson and Linnae Johansson are just a few of the people I'm lucky to have in my life.

BIBLIOGRAPHY

Alou, Felipe with Weiskopf, Herm. *Felipe Alou: My Life and Baseball.* Waco, Texas: Word Books, 1967.

Beitiks, Edvins. "L.A. beaten by flying objects," *San Francisco Examiner,* Sept. 18, 1997.

Bitker, Steve. *The Original San Francisco Giants: The Giants of '58.* Champaign, Illinois: Sports Publishing Inc., 1998.

Bush, David. "Beck shoots out Dodgers' lights," *San Francisco Chronicle,* Sept. 19, 1997.

Bush, David. "Giants win with 6 runs in ninth," *San Francisco Chronicle,* April 27, 1985

Camps, Mark. "Champagne-soaked Giants heap accolades on Clark," *San Francisco Chronicle*, Oct. 10, 1989.

Cepeda, Orlando and Fagen, Herb. *Baby Bull: From Hardball to Hard Time and Back.* Dallas: Taylor Publishing Company, 1998.

Cooper, Tony. "The MVP? It was Clark all the way," *San Francisco Chronicle,* Oct. 10, 1989.

Curiel, Jonathan. "'Wild Thing' gave Clark the usual," *San Francisco Chronicle,* Oct. 10, 1989.

Dewey, Todd. "Persistence paid off for Dallimore," *Anthem View,* June 16, 2004.

Dickey, Glenn. *San Francisco Giants: 40 Years.* San Francisco: Woodford Press, 1997.

Draper, Rich. "Giants come charging back," *Major League Baseball: The Official Site.* www.MLB.com, May 1, 2004.

Dravecky, Dave with Stafford, Tim. *Comeback.* Grand Rapids, Michigan: Zondervan Publishing House, 1990.

BIBLIOGRAPHY

Einstein, Charles. "Greatest day of career," *San Francisco Examiner*, May 1, 1961.

Forman, Sean L. "Baseball-Reference.com – Major League Statistics and Information," *www.baseball-reference.com*, 2006.

Gay, Nancy. "Giants rise up, gain on L.A," *San Francisco Chronicle*, Sept. 18, 1997.

Greene, Jamal K. "Dan Gladden, World Series hero," *Sports Illustrated*, Sept. 27, 1999.

Hertzel, Bob. "Giants' Caveman a throwback to another era," *The Sporting News*, July 16, 1990.

Hodges, Russ and Hirshberg, Al. *My Giants*. Garden City, New York: Doubleday and Company, Inc., 1963.

Hoffman, Jared. "Nen is the master," *The Sporting News*, June 11, 2001.

Jenkins, Bruce. "Legendary Clark tames the Wild Thing," *San Francisco Chronicle*, Oct. 10, 1989.

Jenkins, Bruce. "Lewis leaps into lore of Shea Stadium," *San Francisco Chronicle*, July 25, 1994.

Jenkins, Bruce. "Will's biggest thrill," *San Francisco Chronicle*, Oct. 5, 1999.

Jenkins, Bruce. "Who's on third? Brenly," *San Francisco Chronicle*, June 15, 1999.

Keown, Tim. "Giants and Braves finally go head to head," *San Francisco Chronicle*, Aug. 23, 1993.

Keown, Tim. "Last-gasp homer gives Giants 7-6 win," *San Francisco Chronicle*, Aug. 23, 1993.

Kilgallen, James. "Lonely guys, dolls in li'l old NY," International News Service, April 15, 1958.

Kurkjian, Tim. "A real throwback," *Sports Illustrated*, Sept. 3, 1990.

Luciano, Ron and Fisher, David. *Fall of the Roman Umpire*. New York: Bantam Books, 1986.

Magagnini, Stephen. "The Giants' revenge," *San Francisco Chronicle*, Oct. 4, 1982.

Mays, Willie and Sahadi, Lou. *Say Hey: The Autobiography of Willie Mays.* New York: Pocket Books, 1989.

McGrath, Dan. "Giants knock out the Dodgers, 5-3," *San Francisco Chronicle*, Oct. 4, 1982.

Murphy, Brian. *San Francisco Giants: 50 Years.* San Rafael, California: Insight Editions, 2008.

Neel, Eric. "Robb Nen's last pitch," *espn.com*, Sept. 24, 2005.

Nevius, C.W. "One Giant step toward a pennant," *San Francisco Chronicle*, Sept. 18, 1997.

Padecky, Bob. "Gladden's home run gives Giants 7-6 victory," *The Sacramento Bee*, April 27, 1985.

Peters, Nick. "Brenly: 4 errors, 2 HRs, 4 RBIs," *The Tribune*, Sept. 15, 1986.

Peters, Nick. "Leonard's 2-run homer pulls Giants even," *The Tribune*, Oct. 11, 1987.

Peters, Nick. *Tales from the Giants Dugout.* Champaign, Illinois: Sports Publishing LLC, 2003.

Peters, Nick and Stanton, Martha Jane. *Miracle at Candlestick!* Atlanta, Georgia: Longstreet Press, 1993.

Plaut, David: *Chasing October: The Dodgers-Giants Pennant Race of 1962.* South Bend, Indiana: Diamond Communications, 1994.

Romano, John. "Schmidt's thoughts with mom," *St. Petersburg Times*, Oct. 20, 2002.

Schott, Tom and Peters, Nick. *The Giants Encyclopedia.* Champaign, Illinois: Sports Publishing LLC, 2003.

Schulman, Henry. "Enchanted even-ing," *San Francisco Chronicle*, Oct. 24, 2002.

Schulman, Henry. "Giants leap into NLCS," *San Francisco Chronicle*, Oct. 8, 2002.

Schulman, Henry. "Giants trade Relaford for Bell," *San Francisco Chronicle*, Jan. 26, 2002.

Schulman, Henry. "It's just child's play; rout leaves Giants a win from title," *San Francisco Chronicle*, Oct. 25, 2002.

Schulman, Henry. "Lofton draws Cardinals' ire again after game-winner," *San Francisco Chronicle*, Oct. 16, 2002.

Schulman, Henry. "Overpowering Schmidt, Bonds dominate Cubs," *San Francisco Chronicle*, May 1, 2003.

Schulman, Henry. "Sweeping Giants wake," *San Francisco Chronicle*, Sept. 19, 1997.

Schulman, Henry. "Classic Giants: Uribe's homer sends S.F. to World Series," *San Francisco Chronicle*, Oct. 24, 2010.

Selby, Don. "Rube, rookie trio earn Rig's praise," *San Francisco Examiner*, April 16, 1958.

Slusser, Susan. "Drama at the 'Stick," *The Sacramento Bee*, Aug. 23, 1993.

Shatzkin, Mike and Charlton, Jim. *The Ballplayers: Baseball's Ultimate Biographical Reference.* New York: Arbor House/William Morrow, 1990.

Shea, John and Schulman, Henry. "A game removed, blood still boiling," *San Francisco Chronicle*, Oct. 11, 2002.

Spander, Art. *The Art Spander Collection.* Dallas, Texas: Taylor Publishing Company, 1989.

Stevens, Bob. "Giants champions of the west," *San Francisco Chronicle*, Oct. 1, 1971.

Stevens, Bob. "Juan lurches to 25th in Giant Sweep," *San Francisco Chronicle*, Sept. 7, 1968.

Stevens, Bob. "Mays equals all-time mark," *San Francisco Chronicle*, May 1, 1961.

Steward, Carl. "For San Francisco Giants fans, the past melts away," *San Jose Mercury News*, Nov. 6, 2010.

Sullivan, Bill. "Robinson is the main man – again," *San Jose Mercury News*, Sept. 29, 1987.

Swift, E.M. "Will power," *Sports Illustrated*, May 28, 1990.

Valli, Bob. "Giants bomb Cardinals, defuse them with defensive plays," *The*

Tribune, Oct. 11, 1987.

Walter, Bucky. "A foine day for Irish at Candlestick Park," *San Francisco Examiner*, June 29, 1970.

Walter, Bucky. "Mays: never write us off," *San Francisco Examiner*, Oct. 1, 1971.

Walter, Bucky. "On to the playoffs," *San Francisco Examiner*, Oct. 1, 1971.